USBORNE

IMPROVE
YOUR
ENGLISH

Rachel Bladon, Nicole Irving & Victoria Parker

Designed by Isaac Quaye, Diane Thistlethwaite & Michael W. Wheatley

Illustrated by Kevin Faerber & Colin Mier

**Educational consultants:
Jane Davage, Phillipa Ferst, Angie Graham,
Valerie Munro and George Phillipson**

Edited by Jane Chisholm

With thanks to Corinne Stockley and Rachael Swann

CONTENTS

SPELLING

CONTENTS

Niether or *neither*? *Pursue* or *persue*? After using this book you will have no doubt which are the correct spellings. Don't despair if you think you are a bad speller. Although some find it easier than others, spelling is a skill that can be learned. The fun tests in this book will give you lots of spelling practice. There are also guidelines to help you avoid making mistakes.

User's guide

Each double page in this section focuses on particular spelling problems. Read through the summary of guidelines at the top of each left-hand page, then test your spelling by trying the puzzles which follow. The book has not been designed for writing in, so you will need some paper and a pencil or pen for jotting down your answers. You can check them on pages 28-32. Don't worry if you make mistakes. Just work through the book, then go back to the beginning and try again. You will definitely improve next time.

> Watch out for boxes like this. These contain words for you to learn and test yourself on. Some will be new to you, so have a dictionary handy to check up on what they mean and how to use them.

Why is good spelling necessary?

Spelling is an important skill for many reasons. Above all, it is vital to be able to spell correctly so that you do not confuse your reader. For instance, there are certain words (called homophones) which sound the same, but which have different spellings and meanings.

The cereal was advertised on television.

The serial was advertised on television.

Other spellings are so similar that even a small mistake may make it difficult for your reader to understand you.

The desert was a generous helping of lemon meringue pie.

The dessert was a generous helping of lemon meringue pie.

As your spelling gets better, your writing style will also improve, because you will be able to write with confidence, using a wide range of words to express yourself.

Where does English spelling come from?

Modern English is a mixture of languages. Long ago, the Ancient Britons spoke Celtic, but over the centuries each of the peoples that invaded Britain contributed words from their own languages. For example, *skirt* comes from Old Norse, *index* from Latin, and *garage* from French. More recently, English has been affected by influences such as the growth of travel and trade, the World Wars and the rise of broadcasting. For instance, did you know that the word *shampoo* comes from India, *studio* from Italy, and *parade* from Spain? English is still changing today, in order to express new ideas and experiences.

USEFUL TERMS
What are vowels?

The five letters *a, e, i, o* and *u* are known as vowels. When *y* sounds like "i" (as in *sky*) or "e" (as in *jolly*), it is also considered to be a vowel. The other letters of the alphabet, including *y* as it sounds in *yes*, are called consonants. Each vowel has two sounds: short and long. Say the words below. The blue words have short vowel sounds. The red words have long vowel sounds.

hat   fence   stick   dog   mud

gate   tree   kite   bone   blue

What are syllables?

Many words have more than one vowel sound. Each part of a word which has a separate vowel sound is called a syllable. For example, *dig* has one syllable, *mar/ket* has two syllables, *ex/pen/sive* has three and *in/vis/i/ble* has four. Breaking a word down into syllables often makes spelling easier.

Try counting the syllables in the words on this shopping list, then check your answers with the ones on page 28. Don't look at the number of vowels in each word, as this can be misleading. Just say each word aloud, and count the vowel sounds you hear.

soap
toothpaste
detergent
bread
peanuts
macaroni
coffee
milk
eggs

honey
lemonade
cheese
tomatoes
cauliflower
onions
bananas
oranges

What is stress?

When you say words of more than one syllable, you usually put more emphasis on one syllable than the others. For example, *mar̲ket*, *invi̲sible*, *expe̲nsive*. This emphasis is called stress, or accent.

Read out the words on the shopping list again. Can you hear where the stress lies in each one? Check your answers on page 28.

What makes a spelling correct?

The idea of "correct" spelling is not very old. Until the 18th century, people spelled words however they liked. They even thought nothing of spelling a word in several different ways in the same piece of writing. When the invention of the printing press made written material available to large numbers of people, it became clear that spelling needed to be standardized, so everyone knew exactly what a writer meant. The first English dictionary was written by Samuel Johnson and published in 1755. But the patterns he defined were not always consistent or logical. So today, some words are more difficult to spell than others.

English has continued to change since then, as new words have entered the language and others have dropped out of use. Also, the spelling, pronunciation and meaning of some words have gradually altered. This is why there are differences between British, American and Australian English. You will find that a few words can still be spelled in more than one way (such as gipsy/gypsy). In these cases, use the spelling you find easiest to remember. But if you are surprised by a spelling, always check it. It may be misspelled, or even be a different word. For example, passed and past do not mean the same thing.

Vowel sounds are often spelled in unexpected ways. For example, a long "e" is spelled by *i* in *marine*, but by *y* in *tiny*. Also, many vowel sounds are spelled by two vowels together. For example, *tread* (short "e" spelled *ea*) or *float* (long "o" spelled *oa*). The most common ways of spelling vowel sounds are set out for you here. Look at these examples, then test yourself on the puzzles. You can find the answers on page 28.

a **short** *cat*
   long *plate* *paid* *may*
          steak *weight*
          prey *gauge*

e **short** *set* *dead*
   long *eat* *very* *demon*
          feel *sardine*
          piece *ceiling*

u **short** *duck* *come* *young*
   long *clue* *food* *prune*
          fruit *screw* *do*
          coupon

o **short** *pop* *wasp* *laurel* *cough*
   long *stone* *soap* *toe* *throw*

i **short** *fit* *syrup* *build*
   long *pie* *lime* *sky* *height*

An eye for an *i*

Only a few words end in *i*. These are mostly from other languages. Can you spell some from the clues below? The first letter of each word is given to help you.

1 **Two-piece swimsuit**   B
2 **Trip to see animals in the wild**   S
3 **Thrown at parades**   C
4 **Writing and drawings on public walls**   G
5 **Car with driver**   T
6 **Long, thin pasta**   S
7 **Snow-sport footwear**   S
8 **Short skirt**   M
9 **Beige-green**   K
10 **Type of spicy sausage**   S

Double trouble

Can you guess the half-spelled words in these speech bubbles? Two vowels are missing from each gap.

What b_utiful w_ther!

I h_rd it'll cl_d over and r_n later tod_.

P_ple confuse us bec_se we're so alike.

Your barg_n bl_ j_ns r_lly s_t you.

I've b_n w_ting an h_r for my fr_nd.

I s_d we'd l_ve at the us_l time.

Pl_se can we l_k ar_nd ag_n first?

One vowel short

Which vowel is missing from each of these limericks?

There _nce was a man with the n_ti_n,
T_ live _n a b_at _n the _cean,
But his p__r little daughter,
Quite hated the water,
Because _f the up and d_wn m_ti_n.

1

There was an old woman from B_te,
Who played o_t of t_ne on the fl_te,
The noise was so bad
That it drove her q_ite mad
And left her _nable to toot.

2

There once w_s _ brown cow n_med D_isy,
Who w_s pretty but tot_lly l_zy,
She'd gr_ze in her field,
But no milk would she yield,
_nd this drove the f_rmer quite cr_zy.

3

There was a young woman named Lizz_.
Who kept feeling terribl_ dizz_,
She consulted a doctor,
But he onl_ mocked her,
And said that he found it a m_ster_.

4

There was a young g_rl from Tyree,
Who couldn't count further than three,
She tr_ed and she tr_ed -
But _n va_n. "Oh," she cr_ed,
"Four, f_ve, s_x, _s the problem, you see."

5

Th_r_ onc_ was a young boy named Mik_,
Who rod_ a long way on a bik_,
His l_gs got so sor_,
H_ could cycl_ no mor_,
So inst_ad had to g_t off and hik_.

6

Silent e

Some words end in an *e* which you do not pronounce (such as *same*, *concrete* and *arrive*). This silent *e* is important because it gives the vowel that comes before a long sound. For example, if you add a silent *e* to the ends of *hat*, *bit* and *pet*, they become *hate*, *bite* and *Pete*.

1 Take the silent *e* off each word below. Which words have you now spelled? Do these new words have short or long vowel sounds?

use	note	fate	spite	made
hope	rate	kite	cute	ripe

2 Now add a silent *e* onto these words, and listen how the sound of each one changes.

bar	rag	hug	car	fir
sag	far	par	wag	her

3 Which vowel is missing from each of these words? Do they have short or long vowel sounds?

Chin_se	sh_pe	wh_te	teleph_ne
conf_se	al_ne	prod_ce	al_ve
supp_se	compl_te	esc_pe	h_me
resc_e	comb_ne	b_the	appet_te
celebr_te	am_se	sev_re	supr_me

Here are some words in which the letter *y* acts as a vowel. First, use a dictionary to check any meanings you aren't sure of. Next, test your spelling by reading, covering, then writing each word.

TIDY	LYRIC	STYLE
GOODBYE	DYNAMITE	TYPICAL
SYSTEM	CYCLE	SATISFY
DRY	EYE	BUTTERFLY
HYSTERICAL	CAPACITY	RHYTHM
LYNCH	SYMMETRY	DYNASTY
MERCY	TYRANNY	NYLON
GYMNASIUM	HYPNOTIZE	APPLY
MYTHOLOGY	NAVY	OCCUPY
CYMBALS	SUPPLY	SYRINGE
PYTHON	READY	SHY
SYMPHONY	TYRANT	DYING
EMERGENCY	HYMN	UNITY
CRYSTAL	LUXURY	RHYME
TYPEWRITER	PRETTY	LYNX
PYRAMID	CENTURY	SYNTHETIC
ANONYMOUS	IDYLLIC	TYCOON

The most usual way to make a singular noun (naming word) plural is to add an *s*. For example, *word/words.* But there are some other ways of making plurals which are explained below.

You should NEVER use an apostrophe (') to make a word plural. Apostrophes show the owner of something (such as *my daughter's books*). They also mark missing letters. For example, the *o* in *are not* is replaced by an apostrophe in *aren't.*

ies   If a noun ends in *y*, look at the letter before the *y*. If it is a vowel, just add an *s* (as in *monk**e**y/monkeys*). If it is a consonant, change *y* to *i* and add *es* (as in *ba**b**y/babies*).

ves   To form the plurals of nouns ending in *ff*, add an *s* (as in *cuffs, cliffs*). But for words ending in *f* or *fe*, change the *f* or *fe* to *v* and add *es* (as in *sheaf/shea**ves**, kni**fe**/kni**ves***). Exceptions are: *dwarfs, chiefs, griefs, roofs, proofs, beliefs* and *safes.* Three words can have either spelling: *wharfs/wharves, hoofs/hooves, scarfs/scarves.*

es   To make the plural of nouns which end in *ch, sh, s, ss, x* or *z*, simply add *es*. For example, *torches, dishes, buses, kisses, boxes* and *waltzes.*

oes   To make the plural of words ending in *o*, add *s* if there is a vowel before the final *o* (as in *z**o**o*) or if the word is to do with music (such as *solo* and *soprano*). Also add *s* to *disco* and *photo* (*discos, photos*) and names of peoples, such as *Filipinos.* But when there is a consonant before the final *o* (and the words do not fall into the above categories), add *es*. For example, *pota**t**oes.*

Spies in the skies

Two rival organizations have given their secret agents passwords which end in *y*. One organization's passwords can be made plural by adding an *s*, while the passwords of the other change to *ies*. The agents cannot work out who belongs to which organization. Can you help them by sorting out the passwords into two lists?

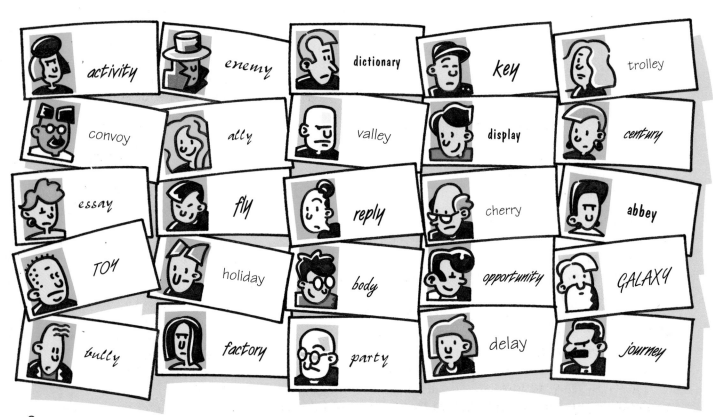

O! What now?

Words which end in *o* have been replaced in this poem with pictures. Can you spell the plurals of these things?

IF I WERE A MARTIAN AND I LIVED IN OUTER SPACE
I'D LIKE TO VISIT EARTH ONE DAY AND LOOK AROUND THE PLACE

I'D LIKE TO MEET AN ▢ AND VISIT HIS ▢

THEN TRAVEL TO AUSTRALIA TO SEE A ▢

I'D ROAM THE VAST AND GRASSY PLAINS TO FIND THE ▢

AND TREMBLE AT THE BOTTOM OF A FIERY ▢

I'D SUFFER FROM ▢ BITES IN HOT EXOTIC LANDS

AND I'D LEARN TO PLAY ▢ AND I'D MARCH WITH BIG BRASS BANDS

I'D HAVE A LITTLE VEGETABLE PATCH WHERE I COULD DIG AND SOW

THEN WATCH ▢ AND ▢ PLANTS TAKE ROOT AND GROW

AND JUST IN CASE ONE DAY I SHOULD FORGET THE THINGS I'D DONE

I'D BE SURE TO TAKE A ▢ OF EACH AND EVERY ONE

SO WHEN THE TIME CAME TO RETURN TO WORK ON MY SPACE STATION
I SHOULD ALWAYS HAVE THESE SOUVENIRS OF MY EARTHLY VACATION

Singularly confused

Words that were originally from other languages often have strange plurals. Do you know how to spell the plurals of the red words in these sentences?

1 I fell asleep on the bus and ended up at the terminus.
2 In the basket of mushrooms I had picked was a poisonous fungus.
3 Another name for a grub that turns into an insect is a larva.
4 My birthday cake was a huge, creamy, chocolate gateau.
5 I looked at the test and realized we had been taught the wrong syllabus.
6 CO₂ is the chemical formula for carbon dioxide.
7 The worst thing to do in a crisis is panic.
8 People's lives can be changed by the medium of television.

F words

In these sentences, words ending in *f*, *fe* and *ff* are singular, but should be plural. Can you spell their plural forms correctly?

1 It took him three puff to blow out the candles on his birthday cake.
2 "Put on scarf, take handkerchief, and behave yourself," their mother said.
3 The hoof of the galloping horses thundered over the race course.
4 Deciduous trees shed their leaf every year.
5 The team played badly in both half of the match.
6 The thief blew open all the safe and escaped with treasures worth millions.
7 It is said that cats have nine life.
8 The shelf were stacked with loaf of bread of all shapes and sizes.
9 At night in the mountains, they could hear wolf howling.
10 King Henry VIII had six wife.
11 Some very modern cars come with sun roof

Plural puzzler

There are a few words which have irregular plurals. For example, one *louse* becomes several *lice*. How many other irregular plurals do you know?

Some nouns, such as *sheep*, stay the same in both the singular and plural. How many more words can you think of like this?

Most sounds in English can be spelled in more than one way. So choosing the right spelling for a pàrticular word can be confusing.

k The sound "k" as in *kid* is sometimes known as hard *c*. It can be spelled as in **c**at, **k**i**ck**, a**cc**ordion, e**ch**o and grotes**que**.

air The sound "air" can be spelled as in **ch**air, sh**are**, b**ear**, th**ere**, th**eir**, and **aer**ial.

sh "sh" sounds can be spelled as in **s**ure, ru**sh**, op**ti**on, i**ss**ue, so**ci**al, an**xi**ous and **ch**ef.

shun A "shun" sound is mostly spelled as in ac**tion**, man**sion**, mi**ssion**, or comple**xion**. But watch out for cu**shion**, fa**shion**, o**cean**, musi**cian** and suspi**cion**.

zhun "zhun" sound is always spelled **sion** (as in occa**sion**), except in words which describe nationality. In these words, "zhun" is spelled **sian** (as in *Asian*, *Malaysian*, *Polynesian*).

er/uh The ends of many English words aren't stressed, so differences between them can be hard to hear. For example, the final syllables of the words *farm**er***, *simil**ar***, *camer**a*** and *act**or*** just sound like "er" or "uh". The sound "er" also occurs in the middle of words. In these cases, it can be spelled as in s**er**ve, **ear**th, b**ir**d, w**or**d, p**ur**se, j**our**ney or Febru**ar**y.

Conquer kicking *k*

Kevin spells all "k" sounds with only the letter *k*. Can you correct his spelling?

I like

Snakes and krokodiles

Hearing my voice eko

Pikniking in the park

Books about shipwreks

Doing magik triks

Klimbing trees

I dislike

Akting in skool plays

Singing in the koir

Losing my train tiket

Stomak-ake

Kornflakes, chiken and brokoli

Kemistry lessons

Are you an *air*-head

There are eleven spelling mistakes in this letter. Can you spot them?

Dear Gran,

My first time on an ereoplane was really exciting - when I'm a millionair I'm going to have my own private jet. My suitcase was bulging - Dad says I'll never have time to where all the clothes and pears of shoes I've brought. But I still managed to forget my hare brush, and Sue's forgotten her teddy bare.

We have a lovely room to shair that looks out on the sea - their are some rair birds to spot along this part of the coast. We're going to a fare tomorrow.

Take cair - we'll see you soon,

Love,

Donna XXXXXXXX

Er ...? Uh ...?

Forgetful Rachel has written two lists to help her remember things. But she has forgotten how to spell "er" and "uh" sounds. Which letters are missing?

THINGS TO BUY:
pizz_, sug_, butt_,
fl_r, tun_, banan_s,
hamburg_s, marm_lade,
chocolate flav_ milkshake,
writing pap_ and env_lopes,
an eras_, a rul_ and a pair
of sciss_s,
2 yards of p_ple ribbon,
film for my camer_,
a package of cake mixt_e,
a batt_y for my calculat_,
a b_thday present
for Samanth_

Rememb_ to take my p_se!

THINGS TO DO:
1 Cut out some pict_es of famous act_s for my project.
2 Sign up for the class trip to the theat_.
3 Ask my next-door neighb_ if I can look for my basketball in his yard.
4 See if my sist_ will let me wear her new dress on Sat_day.
5 Remind Amand_ that it's our t_n this week to look after the _thw_ms in the science room. (Yuk!)

Be sure of *sh*, *shun* and *zhun*

Can you complete this newspaper article by spelling a "sh", "shun" or "zhun" sound to replace each numbered gap?

TRAIN CRASH AND CARRY!

There was a colli..1.. at Spellham Station this morning between two express trains. An electri..2.. carried out an investiga..3.. and reported that an explo..4.. had destroyed signals at a junc..5.. down the line. No one was hurt, but in the confu..6.. two bags of ca..7.. were stolen from one of the trains. The police are an..8..ous to solve this crime quickly, and are appealing for informa..9.. . They have i..10..ued a descrip..11.. of two men seen earlier on the platform, who are now under suspi..12.. . One has a musta..13..e and was disguised as a railway offi..14..al. The other had a worried expre..15.. and a bag with the ini..16..als S.H. on it. They both left together in a ..17..auffeur-driven car.

9

You will almost certainly have seen words spelled with letters that you don't pronounce. These are often letters that used to be pronounced in Old English. For instance, before the 10th century, the *k* in *knot*, the *g* in *gnaw* and the *l* in *folk* were all pronounced. Over the years, the pronunciation of some words changed, while their spellings stayed the same.

So some letters became silent. Other silent letters, such as the *b* in *doubt* and the *p* in *receipt*, were deliberately added during the Renaissance by English scholars. They were trying to make certain words look more like the Latin words they had originally come from.

Here are some common silent letters, showing when they occur:

b "silent" b sometimes occurs after *m* at the end of a syllable or word (as in *plum**b**er* or *clim**b***). It is also found in *de**b**t*, *dou**b**t*, *su**b**tle*.

c can be silent after *s* (as in *s**c**ience* and *s**c**ent*).

k before *n* (as in *k**nife*, *k**not* and *k**nitting*).

g often comes before *n* (as in *g**nome* and *si**g**n*).

h can follow w (as in *w**h**eel*), g (as in *g**h**ostly*), and r (as in *r**h**inoceros*). It is also found at the start of a word (as in *h**onor*), between vowels (as in *ve**h**icle*), and after x, as in *ex**h**ibit*.

l is sometimes silent before d, k or m (as in *shou**l**d*, *wa**l**k* or *sa**l**mon*).

n can be silent after *m* (as in *hym**n***).

w is sometimes silent in front of *h* (as in *w**ho*) and also before *r* at the start of a word (as in *w**rath* and *w**reck*).

p is silent before s, n or t in words which come from Greek (such as *p**neumatic*). It can also be silent after s, as in *ras**p**berry*.

S silent in *i**s**land*, *i**s**le*, *ai**s**le*

t is sometimes silent after s (as in *fas**t**en*).

Tongue twister teasers

Which silent letter is missing from each of these nonsense tongue twisters?

How quickly can you say each one?

1. We wish we were w_ispering w_ales in w_ite w_irling waters.

2. _nomes, _nats and _nus all _nash and _naw _narled nutshells.

3. Fo_k wa_k cha_ky paths ca_mly sta_king quiet qua_mless sa_mon.

4. The _night who _new the _nack of _nitting _nots _nelt with a _nobbly _napsack on the _noll.

5. The clim_ing plum_er's thum_ grew num_.

6. R_yming, r_ythmical r_inoceroses like r_ine-stones and r_ubarb.

7. The _retched _riter _reaked his _rath by _renching the _rinkled _rappers from the _recked _ristwatches.

8. Around the solem_ colum_s the singers' hym_s condem_ed the Autum_.

9. G_ostly g_ouls and g_astly g_osts eat g_erkins in g_oulish g_ettos.

Conversation clues

Which silent letters are missing from the words in these speech bubbles?

W..1..at have you been up to?

Last week I had my pa..2..m read by Madame Rippemovsky, the famous ..3..sychic. I was ag..4..ast at the things she ..5..new. She told me all about my "keep the countryside tidy" campai..6..n, also that I don't like lam..7.. chops or egg yo..8..ks, and that ras..9..berries are the fruit I like most. She ..10..new that I want to be a fashion desi..11..ner and that I'd seen an art ex..12..ibition the day before. She told me that I shou..13..d look for my lost s..14..issors in my brown bag, and also that one day I wou..15..d sail on a ya..16..17..t around forei..18..n and exotic i..19..lands with a tall, dark and han..20..some stranger! I hope she's ri..21..22..t!

Hear this

Certain words have letters which some people pronounce, but others don't, such as the *o* in *factory*. See if you can guess a few of them from these clues. The first letter of each is given to help you. Which are the letters that are often silent?

1	Potatoes, carrots, peas...	V		
2	The month after January	F		
3	A small-scale copy or model	M		
4	Another word for precious	V		
5	The one after eleventh	T		
6	Dark, milk or white	C		
7	Fahrenheit or Centigrade	T		

8	UK politicians assemble here	P
9	Machine for sucking up dust	V
10	This means out of the ordinary	E
11	Custer was a famous one	G
12	A jewel	D
13	Home for monks	M
14	The day after Tuesday	W

The sound of silence

Can you unscramble the jumbled names of the things pictured here?

There is at least one silent letter in each word. Can you spot them?

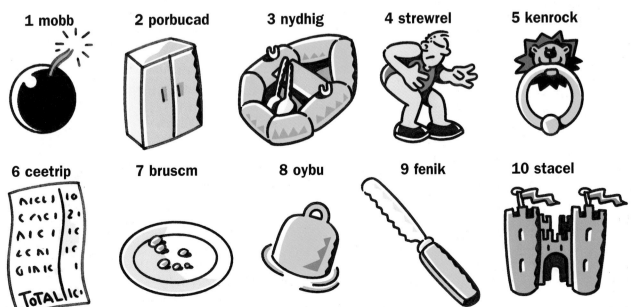

1 mobb   2 porbucad   3 nydhig   4 strewrel   5 kenrock

6 ceetrip   7 bruscm   8 oybu   9 fenik   10 stacel

Some letters regularly occur together in combination. But this can be confusing, as one combination of letters can spell different sounds, while a single sound may be spelled by more than one combination.

gh Combinations such as *ough*, *augh*, and *igh* can be tricky, as the *gh* is heard either as "f" (as in *tough*), or is silent (as in *light*). The most difficult is *ough*, as several sounds are spelled this way.

dge A "j" sound at the end of a word or syllable is spelled *ge* if the vowel sound is long (as in *huge*), or when there is a short vowel with a consonant (as in *cringe*). But if there is a short vowel and no consonant, use *dge* (as in *dredge*). An exception to remember is *pigeon*.

qu After the Norman Conquest, French scribes changed the Old English spelling *cw* to *qu*. For example, *cwic* and *cwen* became *quick* and *queen*. Also, in a few words, they spelled a "k" sound with *que*, as in *picturesque*.

tch Watch out for "ch" sounds at the ends of words or syllables. Where there is a short vowel and no consonant, "ch" is spelled *tch*, as in *catch*. The most common exceptions are: *such*, *much*, *attach*, *detach*, *sandwich* and *bachelor*.

Qu quiz

The king can only reach the queen to deliver his bouquet if he can answer these clues correctly. Can you help him? Begin at number one, and find a word that includes *qu* for each clue. The first letter of each word is given in red.

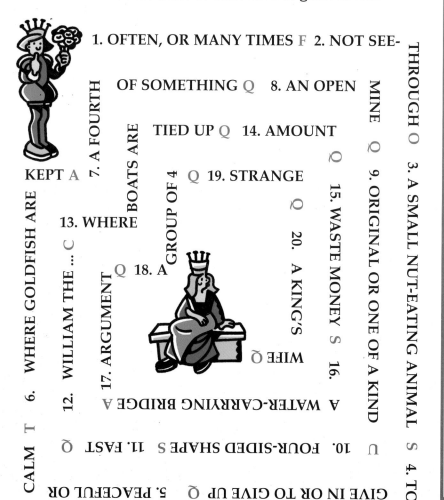

1. OFTEN, OR MANY TIMES F
2. NOT SEE-THROUGH O
3. A SMALL NUT-EATING ANIMAL S
4. TO GIVE IN OR TO GIVE UP Q
5. PEACEFUL OR CALM T
6. WHERE GOLDFISH ARE KEPT A
7. A FOURTH OF SOMETHING Q
8. AN OPEN MINE Q
9. ORIGINAL OR ONE OF A KIND U
10. FOUR-SIDED SHAPE S
11. FAST Q
12. WILLIAM THE ... C
13. WHERE BOATS ARE TIED UP Q
14. AMOUNT Q
15. WASTE MONEY S
16. A WATER-CARRYING BRIDGE A
17. ARGUMENT A
18. A GROUP OF 4 Q
19. STRANGE Q
20. A KING'S WIFE Q

Do you know what all these *qu* words mean? Test your spelling by reading, covering, then writing each one.

QUADRUPED
LACQUER
ACQUIRE
SQUASH
GROTESQUE
QUOTA
ETIQUETTE
QUALIFICATION
QUINTET
EQUILIBRIUM
QUOTATION
MARQUEE
QUALM
INQUISITIVE
QUILL
ACQUAINTANCE
QUEUE
REQUISITION
QUERY
EQUATION
QUINTESSENTIAL
QUALITY
SQUADRON
REQUEST

ge or dge?

The sound "j" is missing from the gaps here. Can you pick the right spelling for each one?

choose ch or tch

You can complete the article below by replacing each gap with either *ch* or *tch*.

Pet show fiasco

A colle..1.. pet show ended in disaster last week. Besides the usual cats and dogs, some rather stran..2.. entrants emer..3..d, including a he..4..hog, a ba..5..r, and a rock in a ca..6..! The ju..7.. (Annie Mall, a local vet) crin..8..d as a cat ate a mouse called Mi..9..t, and a parrot mana..10..d to fly up to a high le..11.., out of reach. Some people began to fi..12..t, and accused the he..13..hog of having fleas. Its angry owner said that such remarks did dreadful dama..14.. to people's ima..15.. of the creatures, and blows were exchan..16..d. In the confusion, a puppy called Smu..17.. ran off with the ba..18.. for first prize, and was later declared the winner.

Ki..1..en Pun..2..-up!

Guests at a local hotel had only sandwi..3..es for lun..4.. today, as chefs Pierre Noir (Fren..5..) and Jan Van Glyk (Du..6..) were fighting. Noir accused Van Glyk of scor..7..ing his ..8..icken dish by swi..9..ing up the oven. Van Glyk said he hadn't tou..10..ed it and Noir was no ma..11.. for him anyway. The waiters wa..12..ed and ..13..eered as Noir ..14..ased Van Glyk, clu..15..ing a bu..16..er's ha..17..et. Van Glyk threw a ba..18.. of eggs at Noir, who then poured ke..19..up over Van Glyk's head. The enraged Van Glyk pun..20..ed Noir, who fell and hit his head on a ben..21.., while Van Glyk pi..22..ed forward, wren..23..ing his ankle. Both needed to be carried on a stre..24..er to an ambulance. The police fe..25..ed them from the hospital, where Noir received ten sti..26..es, and Van Glyk, a pair of cru..27..es.

The gh trap

The combinations *ough*, *augh* and *igh* are missing from these speech bubbles.

But which fits each gap?

Alth_ I like these shoes, they're too h_ and too t_t.

Go thr_ the park and turn r_t. Head for the br_t l_ts.

Come with me. I m_t get lost.

I feel really r_ with this c_ and cold.

I can't help l_ing at the s_t of my n_ty d_ter.

I've had en_ of this bone. It's too t_.

I th_t you were pale.

13

A prefix is a group of letters (such as *inter* or *sub*) which you add onto the beginning of a word to change its meaning. Adding a prefix is quite straightforward - you usually keep all the letters, even if the two you are joining are the same. For example, *dis + satisfied = dissatisfied*, *un + nerve = unnerve*.

But when *all* and *well* are used as prefixes, one *l* is dropped. For example, *all + ways = always*, *well + fare = welfare*. But do not drop an *l* when *well* is used with a hyphen. For example, *well-made* and *well-off*. On these pages you can test yourself on some of the most common prefixes.

Guesswork

Most prefixes come from Latin, Greek and Old English. Knowing what they mean can often help you guess the meaning of a new word. Can you figure out the meaning of each prefix below by looking at the examples?

trans	transplant	transform	transfusion
re	replace	reunion	recapture
hyper	hypersensitive	hypertension	hyperactive
post	postpone	postnatal	postgraduate
micro	microchip	microwave	microscope
circum	circumference	circumnavigate	circumstance
omni	omnipotent	omnivore	omnibus
auto	autobiography	autopilot	automatic
multi	multinational	multimillionaire	multilateral
photo	photograph	photosynthesis	photosensitive
anti	anticlimax	antifreeze	antihero
pre	prehistoric	prejudge	prepayment
extra	extraterrestrial	extrasensory	extraordinary
mono	monorail	monopoly	monologue

Picture this

Use the picture clues to guess the prefixes missing from the words below.

1 -pede

2 -scope

3 -circular

4 -natural

5 -happy

6 -cycle

7 -sphere

8 -national

9 -angles

10 -marine

Singled out

Here are some less common prefixes and their meanings:

Do you know what the following words mean?

ante	before/in front of	1	antebellum
ultra	extreme/beyond	2	ultramodern
pseudo	false	3	pseudonym
demi	half	4	demigod
homo	the same/like	5	homophones
intra	inside/within	6	intravenous
mega	large/great	7	megastar
hypo	too little	8	hypothermia
arch	chief	9	archenemy

14

Matching pairs

Can you make words which match the numbered descriptions by joining the prefixes and words below?

1	below freezing	8	above the ground floor
2	junction	9	not to be relied upon
3	below the earth	10	to come back again
4	naughtiness	11	to overcome something
5	not usual	12	action to avoid danger
6	deceitful, lying	13	happening twice a year
7	against the law	14	too many to count

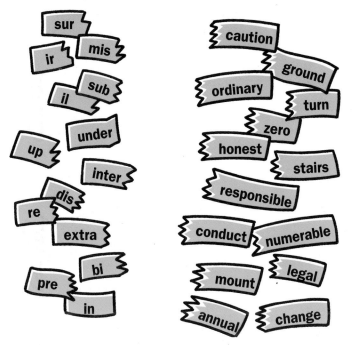

sur, ir, mis, il, sub, under, up, inter, re, dis, extra, bi, pre, in

caution, ground, ordinary, turn, zero, honest, stairs, responsible, conduct, numerable, mount, legal, annual, change

Precise prefixes

Try replacing each of these descriptions with a word that begins with a prefix.

1 lots of different shades
2 to put off until later
3 a self-written life story
4 fluent in two languages
5 an advance showing
6 not cooked enough
7 to vanish
8 to translate a secret message
9 forever
10 to seek out information
11 a disappointing ending
12 not contented
13 unchanging level of sound
14 to change drastically
15 flawed

Face the opposition

Try forming the opposites of the words in capitals below by adding either *un*, *il*, *im*, *mis*, *in*, *ir*, or *dis* onto the front of them.

"How dare you OBEY me!" the king shouted.

Cruelty to animals is completely NECESSARY.

Her writing was so bad it was LEGIBLE.

The 16th century vase I had smashed was REPLACEABLE.

Cats have very DEPENDENT natures.

It is very PROBABLE that we will have snow in August.

Drugs are LEGAL in most countries.

Due to our CALCULATIONS, the carpet was the wrong size.

I could see by the scowl on her face that she APPROVED.

At present, it is POSSIBLE for men to have babies.

"Hurry up! We haven't got all day," she yelled PATIENTLY.

To waste paper is to be environmentally RESPONSIBLE.

We had the FORTUNE to miss each other at the airport.

Although he regretted it, his decision was REVERSIBLE.

In both looks and personality, the twins were SIMILAR.

The MANAGEABLE children ran riot in the classroom.

I used to be DECISIVE, but now I'm not so sure.

It is POLITE to open your mouth while chewing your food.

Soft c

An "s" sound before *i*, *y* or *e* can be spelled with a soft *c*, as in con**c**ept, **c**ylinder and **c**ircumstan**c**e. If a word finishes with a long vowel or a consonant followed by an "s" sound, it is often spelled *ce* (as in tra**c**e and innocen**c**e). This is because *se* at the end of a word usually spells a "z" sound (as in exerci**s**e).

* Exceptions include *tense, precise, collapse, expense, immense, response, suspense* and *sense*.

Hard g

A "g" as it sounds in *green* is known as hard *g*. In certain words, the letter *u* separates a hard *g* from *e* or *i* (as in *guest* and *guide*). Sometimes *u* also separates a hard *g* and the letter *a* (as in *guarantee, guard* and *language*). Certain words end with a hard *g* spelled *gue* (for example, *fatigue, rogue* and *league*.

Soft g

The sound "j" before *e*, *i* or *y* can be spelled with a soft *g*, as in **g**entle, **g**inger and **g**ymnastics. At the ends of words, the sound "jee" is spelled *gy* (as in *biology*) and the sound "idj" is spelled *age* (as in *manage*). *Acknowledge, porridge* and *college* are the most common exceptions to remember.

Endings

Here is a rule for adding endings to words which finish in soft *c* or *g* followed by *e* (like *face* and *stage*). Drop the final *e* if the ending starts with a vowel (*stage + ing + staging*), but keep it if the ending starts with a consonant (*face + less = faceless*). But when adding *ous*, keep *e* after soft *g* (*courage + ous + courageous*), and change it to *i* after soft *c* (*grace + ous = gracious*). Also keep the *e* when adding *able* (as in *peace + able = peaceable*).

Get guessing

Meet private investigator Guy Roper. He puts words containing hard *g* sounds into code. Can you crack it?

Did you 7, 21, 5, 19, 19 it was me?
I'm so good at 4, 9, 19, 7, 21, 9, 19, 9, 14, 7
myself that even my 3, 15, 12, 12, 5, 1, 7, 21, 5, 19
don't recognize me. I 7, 21, 1, 18, 1, 14, 20, 5, 5 I'll
solve any mystery, however 9, 14, 20, 18, 9, 7, 21, 9, 14, 7
it is. If you know where to look, you can always
find clues to 7, 21, 9, 4, 5 you to a
7, 21, 9, 12, 20, 25 person.
At the moment, I'm undercover as a musician -
that's why I have a 7, 21, 9, 20, 1, 18. But unluckily
musical notes are a foreign 12, 1, 14, 7, 21, 1, 7, 5
to me. I have to be on my 7, 21, 1, 18, 4 all the
time so I don't blow my cover.
Shhhh! Someone's coming.
I'd better 7, 5, 20 away ...

Putting an end to it

Can you add endings to the words in capitals, so that the sentences read correctly? Make any spelling changes you think are necessary to alter each word correctly.

1   Gandhi was a **PEACE** man.
2   I'm no good at **SLICE** cake.
3   Our new house is very **SPACE**.
4   His suitcase was **UNMANAGE**.
5   Designer clothes are **OUTRAGE** expensive.
6   I like hot and **SPICE** curries.
7   Bright red is very **NOTICE**.
8   Small oranges are **JUICE**.
9   He **GLANCE** around nervously.
10 The bull was **CHARGE** at me.
11 His **JUDGE** was too harsh.
12 The stain is **SCARCE** visible.
13 Tap **DANCE** is fun.
14 Firefighters are **COURAGE**.
15 Try **BALANCE** on one leg.
16 It is **ADVANTAGE** to speak several languages.

*Turn to pages 26-27 to find out about certain words which end in *ce* when they are nouns, and *se* when they are verbs.

Do you get the gist?

Use these clues to guess words with a soft *g*. The first letter of each is given for you.

1	The study of the Earth, its climate, and how people live	G
2	An animal with a long neck	G
3	A likeness of something or someone, perhaps in a mirror	I
4	Bacteria which make you ill	G
5	Dull, dismal or dirty	D
6	Where a car is kept overnight	G
7	A line down the left side of paper	M
8	Starting point, or beginning	O
9	You give someone this when you say you're sorry to them	A
10	This is in the air you breathe	O
11	What you might call a person selfish with money	S
12	A very tall person	G
13	Used for binding up injuries	B
14	Fierce, wild or primitive	S
15	A very intelligent person	G
16	Wire enclosure for animals	C

Spell soft *c*

In these three advertisements, words with soft *c* have been jumbled up. Can you unscramble them?

1

Crunch-U-Like

Try our new raceel!

WE GUARANTEE YOU'LL LOVE OUR CIPEER OF
crunchy oats and ciyuj stuirc fruit chunks
OR YOUR MONEY BACK!

2

MERRIMAN'S CUCSIR

OPENS AT 8PM WITH A

FACEMINTGIN SICNOSROPE

GAZE AT THE

INOSECRIP OF KNIFE THROWERS
THE NICETRATNOONC OF JUGGLERS
THE CRAGE OF TRAPEZE ARTISTS
THE BLANECA OF HIGH-WIRE WALKERS

GASP IN ECMINXTEET

AS STEVIE STAR SPINS TWO HUNDRED ASCURSE
AND
MARVIN THE MARVELOUS STINYCUILC
MAKES A STEEP ACNEST UP A TIGHTROPE

LAUGH AT THE ENEXTCELL CLOWNS!

BE DEEDVICE BY THE WORLD-FAMOUS MAGICIAN

"THE GREAT MYSTERIO"

SEE THE GREATEST SHOW OF THE TUNRYCE!

3

Sample the ceepa
of
Writington Nature Reserve

A brief film show in our mini-minace rotnudesic
the many different sicpees you can see.

Wander around our curralic nature trail
at your own novinecenec.

Don't forget to visit the swannery, where you can
watch gsnecty and parent swans in their natural habitat

WHY NOT STOP FOR REFRESHMENT AT OUR SELF-VEERSIC CAFE?
SEE YOU SOON!

The ends of many English words are not emphasized. This means that differences can be difficult to hear and so also to spell.

able/ible
The endings *able* and *ible* are often confused, as they both sound and mean the same (to be fit or able to). As *able* is much more common, it's easiest to learn which words end in *ible*. But there are some useful tips to remember.

You usually drop silent *e* when adding *able* or *ible*. For example, *use* + *able* = *usable*, *sense* + *ible* = *sensible*. But remember that after soft *c* or *g* there is an *e* before *able* (for example, *peaceable*, *manageable*), but not before *ible* (*invincible*, *unintelligible*). Also watch out for *soluble*, which has neither *a* nor *i*.

cul
Words which end in the sound "cul" are spelled *cal* if they are adjectives (such as *medical* and *practical*), *cle* if they are nouns (such as *circle*), and sometimes also *kle* (as in tickle and fickle).

ise/ize
You might see some words spelled both *ize* and *ise* (such as *realize /realise*). This is because in the UK both are correct in many cases. In the US, however, *ize* is the usual spelling. But in both countries there are some words which can only be spelled *ise*. These include: *advise, advertise, compromise, despise, devise, disguise, enterprise, exercise, improvise, revise, supervise, surmise, surprise, televise.*

ence/ance
More words end in *ence* or *ent* than *ance* or *ant*. After hard *c* or *g* use *ance/ant* (as in *significance*), but after a soft *c* or *g* use *ence/ent* (as in *negligent*). Watch out for *dependant* - this means a person who is *dependent*, with no *independence*.

---

w*ise* or w*ize*?

The "ize" sounds are missing from these sentences. But how should each one be spelled - *ise* or *ize*?

1 **She was so thin I hardly recogn_d her.**

2 **Exerc_ is good for you.**

3 **The second edition has been rev_d.**

4 **The teacher had 30 children to superv_.**

5 **My friends organ_d a surpr_ party for me.**

6 **The music store special_s in pianos.**

7 **Some snakes hypnot_ their prey.**

8 **The sales assistant pressur_d me into buying it.**

9 **I won first pr_ in the competition.**

10 **Our new puppy was advert_d in the newspaper.**

11 **When the actor forgot his lines, he had to improv_.**

12 **I like taking part, but I desp_ losing.**

13 **My big brother critic_s me.**

14 **I went trick or treating disgu_d as a vampire.**

15 **My brother custom_d his bicycle.**

Probably horrible

Try replacing each numbered gap in this unusual report with either *able* or *ible*.

Last night, I was driving with the roof of my convert..1.. car down, when a strange light became vis..2.. in the sky. It landed in a nearby field, and I set off to investigate. As I drew nearer to the light, a spaceship became recogniz..3.. It wasn't advis..4.. to hang around, but I was unmov..5.. at the terr..6.. sight. Suddenly, a kind of collaps..7.. ladder appeared - whatever horr..8.. things were lurking inside wanted to be soci..9.. I didn't wait to find out if they were peace..10.., but ran for my life. It's understand..11.. if you find my incred..12.. story unbeliev..13.., as I have no reli..14.. proof. But I am sens..15.., respons..16.., and not at all gull..17.. . I never thought life in outer space was poss..18.., but this unforgett..19.. experience has made me change my mind.

Possibly problematical

The clues below describe words which end with a "cul" sound. The first letter of each word is given, to help you guess them. How is each word spelled?

1 What the p stands for in P.E   P
2 Round shape   C
3 Something in your way   O
4 Hanging finger of ice   I
5 Vegetables preserved in vinegar   P
6 Of utmost importance   C

7 Where your foot joins your leg   A
8 A type of music   C
9 Single eye glass   M
10 Cars, trucks etc. are all types of this   V
11 Two-wheeled transportation   B
12 In the surrounding area   L

Trail finder

The letters *a* and *e* are missing from the words in this grid. Starting at the top left arrow, there is an invisible path of *ant* and *ance* words through the surrounding *ent* and *ence* words, leading out at the bottom right arrow*. Can you find this path?

acquaint-nce		resid_nce			excell_nt		accid_nt
confid_nce	clear_nce	cli_nt	differ_nce	serv_nt	adjac_nt	inst_nt	sent_nce
differ_nce	allow_nce	evid_nt	griev_nce	appar_nt	import_nt	obedi_nt	fragr_nt
innoc_nt	ignor_nt	refer_nce	defend_nt	circumfer_nce	frequ_nt	pres_nce	reluct_nce
	sil_nt	ramp_nt			interfer_nce	persever_nce	
	occurr_nce	influ_nce	exist_nce	nuis_nce	impertin_nt	appear_nce	
intellig_nt	perman_nt	assist_nt	appli_nce	viol_nt	disturb_nce	promin_nt	consequ_nce
differ_nce	observ_nt	audi_nce	appar_nt	abs_nce	immin_nt	prud_nt	insol_nce
par_nt	dilig_nt	lieuten_nt	attend_nce	ten_nt	resembl_nce	insur_nce	pret_nce
conveni_nt		effici_nt			consci_nce		ambul_nce

Here are some words which end in *ible*. Do you know what they all mean?

Test your spelling by reading, covering, then writing each one.

EXHAUSTIBLE	CONTEMPTIBLE	IRRESISTIBLE	REVERSIBLE
NEGLIGIBLE	IMPERCEPTIBLE	OSTENSIBLE	PERMISSIBLE
INDIGESTIBLE	SUSCEPTIBLE	TANGIBLE	EXTENDIBLE
DISCERNIBLE	FORCIBLE	INDESTRUCTIBLE	ACCESSIBLE
DIVISIBLE	EDIBLE	FLEXIBLE	INDELIBLE
LEGIBLE	PLAUSIBLE	INCORRIGIBLE	FEASIBLE
DISMISSIBLE	ELIGIBLE	ADMISSIBLE	FALLIBLE
REPREHENSIBLE	INCOMPREHENSIBLE	CORRUPTIBLE	DEDUCTIBLE

*The path can lead horizontally, vertically or diagonally.

A suffix is a letter, or combination of letters, added onto the end of a word to change either the meaning or the way the word is used. You usually need to make some alterations in order to add a suffix.

_e_ If a word ends in silent _e_, drop the _e_ when adding a suffix which begins with a vowel (for example, _examine_ + _ation_ = _examination_). But watch out for _age_ + _ing_, as both _aging_ and _ageing_ are correct. Other exceptions include: _acreage_, _singeing_, _dyeing_, _gluey_, words to which _able_ is added (such as _loveable_), and words ending in soft _c_ or soft _g_ when _ous_ is added (see page 16).

If the suffix begins with a consonant, keep the _e_ (for example, _care_ + _less_ = _careless_). Exceptions to this include: _argue_ + _ment_ = _argument_, _awe_ + _ful_ = _awful_, _due_ + _ly_ = _duly_, _true_ + _ly_ = _truly_, _whole_ + _ly_ = _wholly_.

ous The suffix _ous_ means "full of" (as in _generous_ - full of generosity). When adding _ous_ to _labor_, you need to add an _i_ (_laborious_). Also watch out for words which end in f, as this changes to _v_ when _ous_ is added. For example, _grief/grievous_, _mischief/mischievous_.

_y_ Many people find it confusing to add a suffix to a word ending in _y_. The rule is similar to the one for forming plurals (see page 6). Look at the letter before the _y_. If it is a vowel, just add the suffix. For example, _enjoy_ + _ment_ = _enjoyment_. If it is a consonant, change the _y_ to _i_. For example, _luxury_ + _ous_ = _luxurious_, _heavy_ + _ness_ = _heaviness_, _plenty_ + _ful_ = _plentiful_.

But there are several exceptions to remember. Always keep a final _y_ when adding _ing_. So _bury_ + _ing_ = _burying_, but _bury_ + _ed_ = _buried_. Also keep a final _y_ before adding _ish_ (as in _babyish_), and whenever the _y_ sounds like long "i" (as in _shyly_). When adding the suffix _ous_ to _pity_, _beauty_ and _plenty_, you need to change the final _y_ to _e_, not _i_, as in _piteous_, _beauteous_ and _plenteous_. Also beware of another two exceptions: _joy_ + _ous_ = _joyous_ and _calamity_ + _ous_ = _calamitous_. The letter _y_ unexpectedly changes to _i_ in the following: _lay/laid_, _pay/paid_, _say/said_, _slay/slain_, _day/daily_, _gay/gaily/gaiety_.

How about _ous_?

Try forming adjectives ending in _ous_ from the nouns in capitals below.

1 Modeling is a GLAMOUR profession.

2 Lightning is extremely DANGER

3 Japan is a very MOUNTAIN country.

4 I am reading a HUMOR book.

5 Matthew is a STUDY pupil.

6 I am always ANXIETY to arrive on time.

7 Monkeys are MISCHIEF creatures.

8 Housework is dull and LABOR.

9 A dancer's life demands RIGOR discipline.

10 Be CAUTION when crossing the road.

Now you see it...

Sometimes a letter "disappears" when you add a suffix - usually a vowel in the last syllable. For example, *tiger* + *ess* = *tigress*. Try joining the words and suffixes opposite. You will need to make a letter disappear from each one. (Beware of numbers 8 and 10. You need to make an additional change to each of these.)

1	curious + ity	9	waiter + ess
2	hinder + ance	10	maintain + ance
3	repeat + ition	11	winter + y
4	exclaim + ation	12	explain + ation
5	disaster + ous	13	monster + ous
6	administer + ate	14	vain + ity
7	four + ty	15	remember + ance
8	pronounce + ation	16	nine + th

All's well that ends well

Can you add suffixes to the words in pink here, so that this letter makes sense? You will have to decide what to do with the silent *e* on the end of each word.

Dear Jamal,
I'm WRITE to invite you to my birthday CELEBRATE next Thursday at the AMUSE park. It's still undergoing RENOVATE but will be open from Monday. It'll be very EXCITE. There's an AMAZE water flume and a really SCARE roller coaster. If you're EXTREME DARE, there's also a huge wheel in which you go backward and upside down while REVOLVE sideways. Can you IMAGE it? Even I might not be ADVENTURE enough for that! Dad says he'll do the DRIVE, so don't have an ARGUE with your parents about how you're going to get there and back. I was USE at PERSUADE Dad to come in, too. He thinks it'll be TIRE and NOISE. So, we can go on our own as long as we're on our best BEHAVE and act SENSE. Let me know if you're COME. I'm really HOPE to see you. It should be TRUE awesome.
 Lots of love,
 Miles

P.S. I'm sending INVITE to Tanya and Steve too, but it's LIKE Tanya won't come. She's quite NERVE and says you have to be RIDICULE to enjoy being frightened.

What to do with *y*

Follow these paths to find out which word leads to which suffix. Can you join them correctly? How many other ways can you find of joining these words and suffixes?

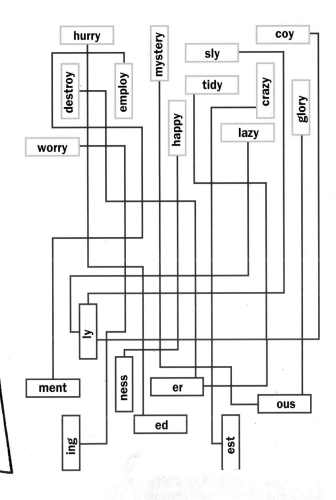

A real hand*ful*

When added as a suffix, *full* is spelled *ful* (as in *helpful*). But the suffix *fully* keeps the double *l* (as in *helpfully*). Here are some more examples:

skillful, spoonfuls, peacefully, beautiful, tasteful, joyfulness, useful, willfully, graceful, forgetfulness. Can you think of any others?

ie/ei Many people have problems spelling words which include *ie* or *ei*. Remembering this rhyme can be helpful:

> I BEFORE E EXCEPT AFTER C-
> BUT ONLY WHERE THESE LETTERS
> SOUND LIKE LONG "E"

For example, the long "e" sound in *believe* is spelled *ie*, but this same sound is spelled *ei* in *perceive* as it occurs after the letter *c*.

There are some exceptions though, the most common of which are *seize*, *weird*, *caffeine*, *species* and *protein*.

But *ie* and *ei* sometimes make sounds other than long "e". For example, *ie* and *ei* can spell a long "i" sound (as in *society* and *height*). *Ei* can also spell a long "a" (as in *weight*), or the sound "air" (as in *their*). Watch out for tricky spellings like these.

i and *e* quick quiz

Use the picture clues to help you unscramble these words. Each one contains *ie* or *ei*.

| 1 ITHEF | 2 HEGIT | 3 WIVE | 4 DIFLE |
| 5 ITE | 6 FRAKEHIDENCH | 7 DILSHE | 8 ROSELID |

Here are some words which include ie and ei. Look them up in a dictionary if you don't know what they mean. Next, test your spelling by reading, covering, then writing each one.

SURFEIT	BELIEF	GAIETY	SIEGE
YIELD	EXPERIENCE	SKEIN	FEINT
RECEIPT	FREIGHT	DIESEL	LIEUTENANT
REIGN	CONCEIT	SIEVE	ACQUIESCE
MEDIEVAL	GRIEVANCE	RETRIEVE	BEIGE
LIE	PERCEIVE	SHEIK	CONSCIENCE
TIER	RELIEF	PIERCE	SERIES
EFFICIENT	WEIR	CEILING	THEIR
CONVENIENT	GEISHA	BIER	QUIET
RECIPIENT	MOVIES	ORIENTAL	RELIEVE
ATHEIST	EIDERDOWN	FIEND	ALIEN
SEISMIC	PIETY	SIENNA	DEITY

Missing pieces

Can you finish off these words correctly? They all include *ie* or *ei*.

1 Mrs. Jones and Mrs. Patel are next-door n_.
2 "Pat_ is a virtue," the p_ told his congregation.
3 The E_ Tower is in Paris.
4 Max is a very diso_ dog.
5 Pirates' gold is also known as "p_ of e_".
6 Santa Claus's s_ is drawn by seven r_.
7 When the portrait was unv_, they all saw it had gone!
8 He was h_ to the throne.

Check up on *ie* and *ei*

The following words are missing from "Fierce Justice": *society*, *reprieve*, *chief*, *brief*, *feigned*, *achievement*, *lenient*. Can you choose the right one to replace each numbered gap? Next, see if you can rearrange the jumbled words in "Tips for Tops" to find Dr. Ivor Cure's hints for a healthy life.

Finally, *ie* and *ei* have been left out of the horoscopes below. But which combination completes each word?

Fierce Justice!

BANK ROBBER SENTENCED TO 125 YEARS

A judge has sentenced two men accused of robbing a bank at gunpoint to 125 years in prison. Throughout their ..1.. trial the men ..2.. innocence, in the hope of a ..3.. But the judge said he could not be ..4.. as the pair were obviously a menace to ..5.. . ..6.. Inspector Lawless said that putting these bad criminals behind bars was a great ..7.. .

TIPS FOR TOPS

1 Make sure your **tide** contains plenty of **tirpone**.
2 Watch your **thewig**.
3 Reduce your cholesterol intake - it's bad for your **seniv**.
4 Drink **dacefatfendie** coffee.
5 Eat a **yearvit** of foods, to make sure you get all the **sunnitret** necessary for good health.

6 Spend some of your **reelius** time each week exercising.
7 Meditate regularly, in order to **reeveil** stress and **texyain**.
8 Make sure you have a bath or shower every day. Personal **heegyin** is very important.

Star spot

Aquarius
You will rec..1..ve a gift.

Pisces
Don't get too t..2..d up with people's problems.

Aries
Have a night out with fr..3..nds.

Taurus
Watch out for counterf..4..t money.

Gemini
The results of a sc..5..ntific experiment will interest you.

Cancer
You will take ..6..ther a boat or plane trip.

Leo
Make a recipe using unusual ingred..7..nts.

Virgo
Don't let a stranger dec..8..ve you.

Libra
S..9..ze the chance for a new exper..10..nce.

Scorpio
It's a good time to begin learning a for..11..gn language.

Sagittarius
Visit some anc..12..nt ruins.

Capricorn
You will hear from a distant relation, perhaps a nephew or n..13..ce.

Words with double letters (such as nece*ss*ary) are confusing to spell. But knowing whether to double a final letter when adding a suffix is even more difficult. It depends on the number of syllables in a word and where the stress lies. There are also special rules for words ending in *r* and *fer*.

one When adding a suffix to a word of one syllable, a short vowel sound and one final consonant* you do not normally double the final letter. For example *worship/worshiped/worshiping*. Watch out for exceptions to this rule such as *gladden, woolly* and *crueller*. If you are unsure, check in a dictionary.

fer In two-syllable words which end in *fer*, the stress sometimes changes from the final syllable to the first syllable when a suffix is added. In these cases, do not double the final *r*. For example, *refer + ee = referee*, *prefer + able = preferable*. When the stress does not change place, use the rule for words ending in *r*. For example, *refer + ing = referring*.

r A final *r* stays single if the stress is on the first syllable (for example, *offer/offering*). If the stress is on the second syllable, double the *r* (for example; *occur/occurring*). But if there are two vowels before the *r*, leave it single (as in *despair/despairing*).

two For two-syllable words which end in one consonant* (such as *pilot*), don't double the final letter if the stress falls on the first syllable (for example, *pilot + ing = piloting*, *gallop + ed = galloped*). When the stress lies on the second syllable, double the final letter if the suffix begins with a vowel, but leave it single if it begins with a consonant. For example, *regret + ing = regretting*, but *regret + fully = regretfully*.

Missing doubles

Double *b, c, d, f, g, l, m, n, p, r, s, t* and *z* are missing from the pages of this story. But which do you need to complete each word?

I had had a fu..1..y feeling about things from the begi..2..ing. I had mi..3..ed my co..4..ection - the last train till morning, so asked someone (a sma..5.. man with a shifty a..6..earance and a nervous ma..7..er) to reco..8..end a hotel. Leaving my lu..9..age, I set off. The weather was ho..10..ible - to..11..ential rain poured down my co..12..ar and co..13..ected in my boots, while the wind whi..14..ed around me. After walking for ages down a deserted road, with no sign of any a..15..o..16..dation, I was ge..17..ing i..18..itable and depre..19..ed. Su..20..enly, I saw da..21..ling headlights coming from the o..22..osite direction. I a..23..empted to a..24..ract the driver's a..25..ention, but the car a..26..elerated as it a..27..roached! I leapt out of the way, just avoiding a co..28..ision, and ho..29..led to the side of the road. Having na..30..owly avoided a te..31..ible a..32..ident, I was also u..33..erly lost. What was I to do? Just then, I noticed a light in the distance. I trudged toward it through the su..34..ounding darkne..35.., over pe..36..les and through pu..37..les of mu..38..y water, until eventua..39..y

I a..40..ived at a sha..41..y li..42..le co..43..age.
I knocked, cautiously, but there was no reply. Su..44..re..45..ing my nerves, I heaved the door open with a great e..46..ort, and ste..47..ed into a dark pa..48..age. On my i..49..ediate right stairs led down - I a..50..ume to the ce..51..ar. An o..52..ensive sme..53.. came wafting up. In a room to my left, a table was set with food and a cup of co..54..ee - still warm. I was pu..55..led as to why the o..56..upant had left in such a hu..57..y. But before I could satisfy my a..58..etite by a..59..acking the food, I realized with a shu..60..er that I was not alone! I turned around to find myself looking down the ba..61..el of a gun. A man with a ha..62..ard expre..63..ion was calmly si..64..ing by the door, behind me. I hoped he didn't have an itchy tri..65..er finger. I could tell he was a profe..66..ional vi..67..ain by the way he said, "Don't make it nece..68..ary for me to shoot you." I didn't like his a..69..itude one bit. But as my mo..70..o is "never say die," I determined to try to escape at the first o..71..ortunity, or find a way to get a me..72..age to someone, somehow.

*When a word ends with two consonants, the final letter always stays single. For example, *start + ed = started, prevent + ing = preventing*.

Watch out for the double letters in these words:

ACCURATE
VACCINATE
PROFESSION
IRRITATE
DESICCATE
SUGGEST
POSSESS
AGGRESSION
EMBARRASS
ADDRESS
INFLAMMABLE
DISSECT
APPLAUSE
ACCURATE
CORRESPOND
NECESSARY
ERROR
ASSESS
COMMAND
QUESTIONNAIRE
COMMUNICATION
EXAGGERATE
INTERRUPT
DISAPPOINT
ECCENTRIC
INTERROGATE
SUCCEED
PARALLEL

Doubling decisions

Here is an interview with Bob Barley, singer with The Howlers. To make it read correctly, try adding an ending to each word in capitals. But watch out for any letters that need to be doubled.

Q How did you become a star?
A I can DIM remember asking for a guitar when I was three. I SHOW that I was REAL talented as soon as I START playing.

Q Have you had any setbacks?
A In the BEGIN things moved SLOW and I had HARD any money. But FAIL never CROSS my mind. I GRAB the chance of RECORD my first single, "I'm FALL for you babe", and I never LOOK back.

Q What do you like best about your job?
A TRAVEL the world and SING live. HEAR the crowd CHEER at the OPEN of a concert is the GREAT FEEL in the world, man.

Q How do you like to spend Sunday?
A STAY in bed and FLIP through the newspapers while SIP a cup of coffee.

Q What's the worst aspect of being famous?
A Being SPOT by fans and MOB wherever I go.

Q Do you ever think of QUIT the business?
A As I get OLD, I do think about STEP down and LET the youngsters take over. But although my hair's GET THIN, I'm not giving up yet.

Q When can we expect a new album from The Howlers?
A We've just SCRAP our latest material to try a change of direction. We're JAM in the studio at the moment.

Q What's your DEEP fear?
A DROP out of the charts and my fans FORGET me.

Q What are your REMAIN aims?
A I want to be an even BIG star!

Problem patterns

Here are some difficult spelling patterns. Look at the base word, then decide whether the missing consonants should be single or double in the words which follow.

1	deter	dete_ed	7	common	commo_er	12	cruel	crue_er
		dete_ing			commo_est			crue_est
		dete_ent			commo_ess			crue_y
2	fit	fi_est	8	bat	ba_er			crue_ty
		fi_ing			ba_ed	13	star	sta_dom
		fi_fully			ba_ing			sta_ed
3	open	ope_er	9	forget	forge_able			sta_ing
		ope_ing			forge_ing	14	commission	commissio_er
		ope_ess			forge_ful			commissio_ing
4	model	mode_ed	10	commit	commi_ee	15	defer	defe_ed
		mode_ing			commi_ing			defe_ing
5	occasion	occasio_al			commi_ment			defe_ment
		occasio_ally	11	occur	occu_ed			defe_able
6	hop	ho_ed			occu_ing	16	happen	happe_ing
		ho_ing			occu_ence			happe_ed

Here are some especially difficult tests. If you can answer all these correctly, you can be sure that you are an excellent speller!

c or s?

A few words are spelled with *c* when they are nouns, but with *s* when verbs. For example, *advice* and *advise*, *device* and *devise*, *prophecy* and *prophesy*. Notice how the pronunciation changes slightly with the spelling. This will help you choose the correct spelling for the way the word is being used.

there/there's/their/theirs/they're

These spellings are very often confused. *There* is the opposite of *here*. *Their* and *theirs* show ownership (for example, *their books*, and *the books are theirs*). *They're* is short for *they are*. *There's* can mean two things: it is usually short for *there is*, but when followed by *been*, it is a short form of *there has*.

Homophones

Homophones are words which sound the same, but which have different spellings and meanings. For example, *there*, *their* and *they're*; *no* and *know*; *past* and *passed*; *threw* and *through*.

Watch out for words which have an "f" sound spelled *ph*. Here are some for you to test yourself on.

PHASE
ORPHAN
PHOBIA
GRAPH
CENOTAPH
PHYSIQUE
EPITAPH
SPHERE
ELEPHANT
PHONOGRAM
PHANTOM
NEPHEW
MICROPHONE
NYMPH
PHRASE
PARAGRAPH
PHEASANT
PHLEGM
CATASTROPHE
METAPHOR
PAMPHLET
PARAPHERNALIA
APOSTROPHE
PHARMACY
PHENOMENON
PHYSIOTHERAPY
DIAPHRAGM

Can you do better?

Here is Ike Canspellit's report card. His teachers have made a lot of spelling mistakes - can you spot them all?

Subject	Name *Ike Canspellit* Class *Upper 4* Comments	Grade
SPORTS	Ike is skillfull on the football feeld and in the swiming pool.	B+
MUSIC	More self-disiplin and practise are neccesary, but Ike has a good scents of rithum.	C
DRAMA	IKE INJOYS BOTH TRADGEDY AND COMIDY AND IS A TALENTED CARACTER ACTER.	B
MATH	Ike has benifitted from atending extra classes. He has definitely improoved, but still makes fawlts threw carelesness	C+
JOGRAPHY	Ike's prodject on equitorial rain forrest's was very nollidgible.	B-
SCIENCE	Ike is unintrested in sience and looses consentration easily. He also displays a tendancy to talk. During practicle work in the laboratory he medals with the ecqipment. His technecks are very disapointing.	D
HISTRY	Ike has a thurugh under standing of the Ainshent World, espeshally of the lifes of the Roman emperors. He has enjoyed lerning about the gods and godeses of Greek mitholojee.	A-
INGLISH	Altho Ike makes littel errers in his grammer, his creativ riting is genrally exsellent. His discriptions are perseptive and ofen humorus. We have been greatful for his asistence in the libry this year. As usuall, Ike is top of the class at spelling.	A+

Signature *Ms V. Unfriendly*   Date *July 1st*

Noun or verb?

Try replacing each of the gaps in these sentences with either *c* or *s*. In order to pick the right spelling, you need to decide whether each word with a missing letter is a noun or a verb.

1 He had devi_ed a cunning plan.
2 I advi_ed her not to give up trying.
3 Whoever devi_ed the alarm clock was very clever. It is a useful devi_e.
4 A clairvoyant prophe_ied my future, but I will be very surprised if her prophe_y comes true.
5 She took absolutely no notice of my excellent advi_e.

Sound-alike

Can you pick the correct spellings from the homophones on this page of Wendy's diary?

5th April

The weather/whether today was fowl/foul, but I'd promised to meat/meet Grandad at half passed/past two/to/too. He was already/all ready there. He waived/waved when he saw/sore me. He said he'd only had a short wait/weight. He asked if I'd mist/missed him - of course /coarse! It was poring/pouring with rain, but we wandered/wondered along the beach/beech anyway. He said I'd groan/grown since he'd last scene/seen me - what a complement /compliment! I said he should try dyeing/dying his white hair/hare. He laughed, and tolled/told me that he hated the whole/hole business of

Saturday

getting old. He said it seemed only yesterday when he used to read bedtime stories/storeys aloud /allowed to me. We talked about how board/bored I am at school. Grandad said I should no/know that every lessen/lesson is important, and that my opinion will alter/altar. That maybe/may be sow/so/sew, but I'm shore/sure I'll never enjoy chemistry! I led/lead the way to the station to ensure/insure that he didn't get lost. He asked me to right/write soon, and gave me some stationery/stationary with my name and address at the top of every peace/piece of paper.

Can you get *there*?

Can you think of shorter ways to say the underlined parts of these sentences?

You will have to use *there*, *there's*, *their*, t*heirs*, or *they're* in each one.

1 Look! There is Michelle!
2 Look at that, over in that direction!
3 I know they are going away today.
4 The house belonging to them is huge.
5 I want one just like the one they have.
6 There has been a dreadful accident.

7 Drop it! It's the one belonging to them.
8 There has been a snowfall overnight.
9 I liked the friends belonging to them.
10 Have some more. There is plenty left.
11 I hate going to that place.
12 They are always arguing.

The final frontier

Here are just a few of the most commonly misspelled words. Why not make your own list of difficult spellings?

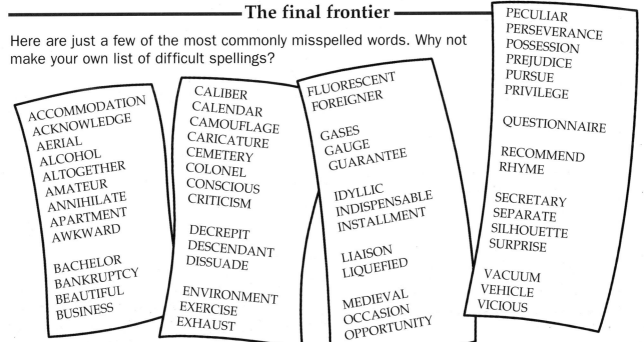

ACCOMMODATION
ACKNOWLEDGE
AERIAL
ALCOHOL
ALTOGETHER
AMATEUR
ANNIHILATE
APARTMENT
AWKWARD

BACHELOR
BANKRUPTCY
BEAUTIFUL
BUSINESS

CALIBER
CALENDAR
CAMOUFLAGE
CARICATURE
CEMETERY
COLONEL
CONSCIOUS
CRITICISM

DECREPIT
DESCENDANT
DISSUADE

ENVIRONMENT
EXERCISE
EXHAUST

FLUORESCENT
FOREIGNER

GASES
GAUGE
GUARANTEE

IDYLLIC
INDISPENSABLE
INSTALLMENT

LIAISON
LIQUEFIED

MEDIEVAL
OCCASION
OPPORTUNITY

PECULIAR
PERSEVERANCE
POSSESSION
PREJUDICE
PURSUE
PRIVILEGE

QUESTIONNAIRE

RECOMMEND
RHYME

SECRETARY
SEPARATE
SILHOUETTE
SURPRISE

VACUUM
VEHICLE
VICIOUS

Page 3

What are syllables?

one syllable:	soap, bread, milk, eggs, cheese
two syllables:	tooth/paste, pea/nuts, cof/fee, hon/ey, on/ions
three syllables:	de/ter/gent, lem/on/ade, to/ma/toes, ba/na/nas, or/an/ges
four syllables:	mac/a/ro/ni, cau/li/flow/er

What is stress?

tooth/paste, *pea*/nuts, *hon*/ey, *cof*/fee, *on*/ions, de/*ter*/gent, lem/on/*ade*, to/*ma*/toes, ba/*na*/nas, *or*/an/ges, mac/a/*ro*/ni, *cau*/li/flow/er

---

Pages 4-5

An eye for an *i*

1 bikini	3 confetti	5 taxi	7 ski	9 khaki
2 safari	4 graffiti	6 spaghetti	8 mini	10 salami

Double trouble

What beautiful weather!

I heard it'll cloud over and rain later today.

People confuse us because we're so alike.

Your bargain blue jeans really suit you.

I've been waiting an hour for my friend.

I said we'd leave at the usual time.

Please can we look around again first?

One vowel short

1 *o* is the missing vowel
2 *u* is the missing vowel
3 *a* is the missing vowel
4 *y* is the missing vowel
5 *i* is the missing vowel
6 *e* is the missing vowel

Silent *e*

1 The new words are:
us, not, fat, spit, mad, hop, rat, kit, cut, rip
These all have short vowel sounds.

2 The new words are:
bare, rage, huge, care, fire, sage, fare, pare, wage, here

3 The completed words are:
Chinese, shape, white, telephone, confuse, alone, produce, alive, suppose, complete, escape, home, rescue, combine, bathe, appetite, celebrate, amuse, severe, supreme
These vowels all have long sounds because of the silent *e* on the end of each word.

Pages 6-7

Sp*ies* in the sk*ies*

the *ys* organization:
convoys, essays, toys, holidays, valleys, keys, displays, delays, trolleys, abbeys, journeys

the *ies* organization:
activities, bullies, enemies, allies, flies, factories, dictionaries, replies, bodies, parties, cherries, opportunities, centuries, galaxies

O! What now?

Eskimo/Eskimo**s**	mosquito/mosquito**es**
igloo/igloo**s**	piano/piano**s**
kangaroo/kangaroo**s**	potato/potato**es**
buffalo/buffalo**es**	tomato/tomato**es**
volcano/volcano**es**	photo/photo**s**

Singularly confused

1 termini	4 gateaux	6 formulae
2 fungi	5 syllabi or	7 crises
3 larvae	syllabuses	8 media

F words

1 puff**s**	6 thie**ves**, safe**s**
2 scarf**s** or scar**ves**, handkerchief**s**, yoursel**ves**	7 li**ves**
3 hoof**s** or hoo**ves**	8 shel**ves**, loa**ves**
4 lea**ves**	9 wol**ves**
5 hal**ves**	10 wi**ves**
	11 roof**s**

Plural puzzler

Irregular plurals include:
mice, men, women, geese, children, teeth, feet
Words that are the same in both the singular and the plural include:
deer, salmon, trout, grouse, moose, news, pants, tights, trousers, scissors, fish, mathematics, series, species, innings

---

Pages 8-9

Er...? Uh...?

THINGS TO BUY:
pizza, sugar, butter, flour, tuna, bananas, hamburgers, marmalade, chocolate flavor milkshake, writing paper and envelopes, an eraser, a ruler and a pair of scissors,
2 yards of purple ribbon, film for my camera, a package of cake mixture, a battery for my calculator, a birthday present for Samantha

Remember to take my purse!

THINGS TO DO:
1 Cut out some pictures of famous actors for my project.
2 Sign up for the class trip to the theater.
3 Ask my next-door neighbor if I can look for my basketball in his yard.
4 See if my sister will let me wear her new dress on Saturday.
5 Remind Amanda that it's our turn this week to look after the earthworms in the science room. (Yuk!)

Conquer kicking *k*

Kevin likes:
snakes and **c**rocodiles
hearing his voice e**ch**o
pi**cn**i**ck**ing in the park
books about shipwre**ck**s
doing magi**c** tri**ck**s
climbing trees

Kevin dislikes:
a**c**ting in s**ch**ool plays
singing in the **ch**oir
losing his train ti**ck**et
stoma**chache**
cornflakes, **ch**i**ck**en
and bro**cc**oli
chemistry lessons

Are you an *air*-head?

Dear Gran,

My first time on an **ai**rplane was really exciting - when I'm a million**ai**re I'm going to have my own private jet. My suitcase was bulging - Dad says I'll never have time to w**ear** all the clothes and pairs of shoes I've brought. But I still managed to forget my h**ai**r brush, and Sue's forgotten her teddy b**ear**.
We have a lovely room to sh**are** that looks out on the sea - there are some r**are** birds to spot along this part of the coast.
We're going to a f**air** tomorrow.
Take c**are** - we'll see you soon,
Love,
Donna XXXXXXXX

Be sure of *sh, shun* and *zhun*

1 colli**sion**
2 electri**cian**
3 investiga**tion**
4 explo**sion**
5 junc**tion**
6 confu**sion**
7 ca**sh**
8 an**xious**
9 informa**tion**
10 is**sued**
11 descrip**tion**
12 suspi**cion**
13 musta**che**
14 offi**cial**
15 expre**ssion**
16 ini**tials**
17 **ch**auffeur

Pages 10-11

Tongue twister teasers

1 h   2 g   3 l   4 k   5 b   6 h   7 w   8 n   9 h

Conversation clues

1 **wh**at
2 pa**l**m
3 **p**sychic
4 a**gh**ast
5 **k**new
6 campai**gn**
7 lam**b**
8 yo**l**k
9 ra**sp**berries
10 **k**new
11 desi**gn**er
12 exhi**b**ition
13 shou**l**d
14 s**c**issors
15 wou**l**d
16/17 ya**ch**t
18 forei**gn**
19 i**s**lands
20 hand**s**ome
21/22 ri**gh**t

Hear this

1 vege**t**able
2 Feb**r**uary
3 mini**a**ture
4 valu**a**ble
5 twel**f**th
6 choco**l**ate
7 tempe**r**ature
8 parli**a**ment
9 vacu**u**m
10 extra**o**rdinary
11 gene**r**al
12 dia**m**ond
13 monas**t**ery
14 We**d**nesday

The sound of silence

1 bom**b**
2 cup**b**oard
3 din**gh**y
4 **w**restler
5 **k**nocker
6 recei**p**t
7 crum**b**s
8 bu**o**y
9 **k**nife
10 cas**t**le

Pages 12-13

Qu quiz

1 fre**qu**ent
2 opa**que**
3 s**qu**irrel
4 **qu**it
5 tran**qu**il
6 a**qu**arium
7 **qu**arter
8 **qu**arry
9 uni**que**
10 s**qu**are
11 **qu**ick
12 con**qu**eror
13 **qu**ay
14 **qu**antity
15 s**qu**ander

16 a**qu**educt
17 **qu**arrel
18 **qu**artet
19 **qu**eer
20 **qu**een

ge or *dge*?

1 colle**ge**
2 stran**ge**
3 emer**ged**
4 he**dge**hog
5 ba**dge**r
6 ca**ge**
7 ju**dge**
8 crin**ged**
9 Mi**dge**t
10 mana**ged**
11 le**dge**
12 fi**dge**t
13 he**dge**hog
14 dama**ge**
15 ima**ge**
16 exchan**ged**
17 Smu**dge**
18 ba**dge**

Choose *ch* or *tch*

1 Kit**ch**en
2 Pun**ch**-up
3 sandwi**ch**es
4 lun**ch**
5 Fren**ch**
6 Dut**ch**
7 scor**ch**ing
8 **ch**icken
9 swi**tch**ing
10 tou**ch**ed
11 ma**tch**
12 wat**ch**ed
13 **ch**eered
14 **ch**ased
15 clu**tch**ing
16 bu**tch**er's
17 ha**tch**et
18 ba**tch**
19 ket**ch**up
20 pun**ch**ed
21 ben**ch**
22 pi**tch**ed
23 wren**ch**ing
24 stret**ch**er
25 fet**ch**ed
26 sti**tch**es
27 cru**tch**es

the *gh* trap

Pages 14-15

Guesswork

trans	across/beyond	**auto**	self
re	again	**multi**	many/much
hyper	too much	**photo**	light
post	after	**anti**	against/opposing
micro	very small	**pre**	before
circum	around	**extra**	beyond/outside
omni	all	**mono**	single

Singled out

1 antebellum - before the Civil War
2 ultramodern - extremely modern
3 pseudonym - a false name, such as used by an author
4 demigod - a half-human, half-immortal being
5 homophones - words which sound the same
6 intravenous - within a vein
7 megastar - a very famous personality
8 hypothermia - abnormally low body temperature
9 arch enemy - chief enemy

Pages 14-15 continued

Picture this

1	centi	3	semi	5	un	7	hemi	9	tri
2	tele	4	super	6	bi	8	inter	10	sub

Matching pairs

1	subzero	6	dishonest	11	surmount
2	interchange	7	illegal	12	precaution
3	underground	8	upstairs	13	biannual
4	misconduct	9	irresponsible	14	innumerable
5	extraordinary	10	return		

Precise prefixes

1	multicolored	6	underdone	11	anticlimax
2	postpone	7	disappear	12	dissatisfied
3	autobiography	8	decode	13	monotone
4	bilingual	9	always	14	transform
5	preview	10	research	15	imperfect

Face the opposition

disobey, unnecessary, illegible, irreplaceable, independent, improbable, illegal, miscalculations, disapproved, impossible, impatiently, irresponsible, misfortune, irreversible, dissimilar, unmanageable, indecisive, impolite

Pages 16-17

Get guessing

Did you **guess** it was me?
I'm so good at **disguising** myself that even my **colleagues** don't recognize me. I **guarantee** I'll solve any mystery, however **intriguing** it is. If you know where to look, you can always find clues to **guide** you to a **guilty** person.
At the moment, I'm undercover as a musician - that's why I have a **guitar**. But unluckily, musical notes are a foreign **language** to me. I have to be on my **guard** all the time so I don't blow my cover.
Shhhh! Someone's coming.
I'd better **get** away...

Putting an end to it

1	peaceable or peaceful	9	glanced
2	slicing	10	charging
3	spacious	11	judgement or judgment
4	unmanageable	12	scarcely
5	outrageously	13	dancing
6	spicy	14	courageous
7	noticeable	15	balancing
8	juicy	16	advantageous

Do you get the gist?

1	geography	7	margin	13	bandage
2	giraffe	8	origin	14	savage
3	image	9	apology	15	genius
4	germs	10	oxygen	16	cage
5	dingy	11	stingy		
6	garage	12	giant		

Spell soft *c*

1 Crunch-U-Like. Try our new **cereal**!
We guarantee you'll love our **recipe** of crunchy oats and **juicy citrus** fruit chunks or your money back.

2 Merriman's **Circus** opens at 8pm with a **magnificent procession**.
Gaze at the **precision** of knife throwers, the **concentration** of jugglers, the **grace** of trapeze artists, the **balance** of high-wire walkers.
Gasp in **excitement** as Stevie Star spins two hundred **saucers** and Marvin the Marvelous **unicyclist** makes a steep **ascent** up a tightrope.
Laugh at the **excellent** clowns!
Be **deceived** by the world-famous magician "the Great Mysterio".
See the greatest show of the **century**.

3 Sample the **peace** of Writington Nature Reserve.
A brief film show in our mini-**cinema introduces** the many different **species** you can see.
Wander around our **circular** nature trail at your own **convenience**.
Don't forget to visit the swannery where you can watch **cygnets** and parent swans in their natural habitat.
Why not stop for refreshment at our self-**service** café? See you soon!

Pages 18-19

wise or *wize*?

1	recognized	6	specializes	12	despise
2	exercise	7	hypnotize	13	criticizes
3	revised	8	pressurized	14	disguised
4	supervise	9	prize	15	customized
5	organized/ surprise	10	advertised		
		11	improvise		

Probably horrible

1	convert**ible**	8	horr**ible**	15	sens**ible**
2	vis**ible**	9	soci**able**	16	respons**ible**
3	recogniz**able**	10	peace**able**	17	gull**ible**
4	advis**able**	11	understand**able**	18	poss**ible**
5	unmov**able**	12	incred**ible**	19	unforgett**able**
6	terr**ible**	13	unbeliev**able**		
7	collaps**ible**	14	reli**able**		

Possibly problematical

1	physi**cal**	5	pic**kle**	9	mono**cle**
2	cir**cle**	6	criti**cal**	10	vehi**cle**
3	obsta**cle**	7	an**kle**	11	bicy**cle**
4	ici**cle**	8	classi**cal**	12	lo**cal**

Trail finder

The letter *a* is missing from: acquaintance, clearance, allowance, ignorant, rampant, defendant, grievance, servant, important, instant, fragrant, reluctance, perseverance, appearance, disturbance, nuisance, appliance, assistant, observant, lieutenant, attendance, tenant, resemblance, insurance, ambulance. The letter *e* is missing from all the other words in the grid. The path looks like this:

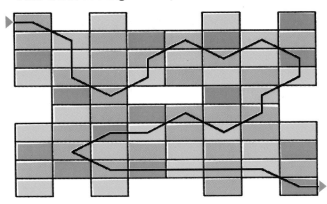

What to do with *y*

worry + ing = worrying	sly + ly = slyly
destroy + er = destroyer	tidy + er = tidier
hurry + ed = hurried	lazy + ly = lazily
employ + ment = employment	crazy + est = craziest
mystery + ous = mysterious	coy + ly = coyly
happy + ness = happiness	glory + ous = glorious

Other possible combinations are: worrier, worried, destroying, destroyed, hurrying, hurriedly, employer, employing, employed, mysteriously, happier, happily, happiest, tidily, tidying, tidiest, tidied, tidiness, slyest, slyness, crazier, crazily, craziness, crazied, lazier, laziest, laziness, glorying, gloried, drying, dried, drier, driest, dryness

========== **Pages 22-23** ==========

i and *e* quick quiz

1	th**ie**f	4	f**ie**ld	7	sh**ie**ld
2	**ei**ght	5	t**ie**	8	sold**ie**r
3	v**ie**w	6	handkerch**ie**f		

Missing p*ie*ces

1	n**ei**ghbors	4	disob**ei**dent	7	unv**ei**led
2	pat**ie**nce	5	p**ie**ces of **ei**ght	8	h**ei**r
	pr**ie**st	6	sl**ei**gh,		
3	**Ei**ffel		r**ei**ndeer		

Fierce Justice

1	br**ie**f	4	len**ie**nt	7	ach**ie**vement
2	f**ei**gned	5	soc**ie**ty		
3	repr**ie**ve	6	ch**ie**f		

Tips for Tops

1	prot**ei**n	4	decaff**ei**nated	7	rel**ie**ve,
2	w**ei**ght	5	var**ie**ty, nutr**ie**nts		anx**ie**ty
3	v**ei**ns	6	l**ei**sure	8	hyg**ie**ne

Star Spot

1	rec**ei**ve	6	**ei**ther	11	for**ei**gn
2	t**ie**d	7	ingred**ie**nts	12	anc**ie**nt
3	fr**ie**nds	8	dec**ei**ve	13	n**ie**ce
4	counterf**ei**t	9	s**ei**ze		
5	sc**ie**ntific	10	exper**ie**nce		

========== **Pages 20-21** ==========

How about *ous*?

1	glamorous	5	studious	9	rigorous
2	dangerous	6	anxious	10	cautious
3	mountainous	7	mischievous		
4	humorous	8	laborious		

Now you see it...

1	curiosity	7	forty	13	monstrous
2	hindrance	8	pronunciation	14	vanity
3	repetition	9	waitress	15	remembrance
4	exclamation	10	maintenance	16	ninth
5	disastrous	11	wintry		
6	administrate	12	explanation		

All's well that ends well

writing, celebration, amusement, renovation, exciting, amazing, scary, extremely, daring, revolving, imagine, adventurous, driving, argument, useless, persuading, tiring, noisy, behavior, sensibly, coming, hoping, truly, invitations, likely, nervous, ridiculous

========== **Pages 24-25** ==========

Missing doubles

1	fu**nn**y	5	sma**ll**	9	lu**gg**age
2	begi**nn**ing	6	a**pp**earance	10	ho**rr**ible
3	mi**ss**ed	7	ma**nn**er	11	to**rr**ential
4	co**nn**ection	8	reco**mm**end	12	co**ll**ar

Pages 24-25 continued

13 collected	33 utterly	53 smell
14 whipped	34 surrounding	54 coffee
15/16	35 darkness	55 puzzled
accommodation	36 pebbles	56 occupant
17 getting	37 puddles	57 hurry
18 irritable	38 muddy	58 appetite
19 depressed	39 eventually	59 attacking
20 suddenly	40 arrived	60 shudder
21 dazzling	41 shabby	61 barrel
22 opposite	42 little	62 haggard
23 attempted	43 cottage	63 expression
24 attract	44/45	64 sitting
25 attention	suppressing	65 trigger
26 accelerated	46 effort	66 professional
27 approached	47 stepped	67 villain
28 collision	48 passage	68 necessary
29 hobbled	49 immediate	69 attitude
30 narrowly	50 assume	70 motto
31 terrible	51 cellar	71 opportunity
32 accident	52 offensive	72 message

Doubling decisions

dimly, showed, really, started, beginning, slowly, hardly, failure/failing, crossed, grabbed, recording, falling, looked, traveling, singing, hearing, cheering, opening, greatest, feeling, staying, flipping, sipping, spotted, mobbed, quitting, older, stepping, letting, getting, thinner, scrapped, jamming, deepest, dropping, forgetting, remaining, bigger

Problem patterns

1 deterred	deterring	deterrent
2 fittest	fitting	fitfully
3 opener	opening	openness
4 modeled	modeling	
5 occasional	occasionally	
6 hopped	hopping	
7 commoner	commonest	commonness
8 batter	batted	batting
9 forgettable	forgetting	forgetful
10 committee	committing	commitment
11 occurred	occurring	occurrence
12 crueller	cruellest	cruelly
cruelty		
13 stardom	starred	starring
14 commissioner	commissioning	
15 deferred	deferring	deferment
deferrable		
16 happening	happened	

Pages 26-27

Noun or verb?

1 He had devised a cunning plan.
2 I advised her not to give up trying.
3 Whoever devised the alarm clock was very clever. It is a useful device.
4 A clairvoyant prophesied my future, but I will be surprised if her prophecy comes true.
5 She took absolutely no notice of my excellent advice.

Sound-alike

weather, foul, meet, past, two, already, waved, saw, wait, missed, course, pouring, wandered, beach, grown, seen, compliment, dyeing, hair, told, whole, stories, aloud, bored, know, lesson, alter, may be, so, sure, led, ensure, write, stationery, piece

Can you do better?

SPORTS   Ike is skillful on the football field and in the swimming pool.

MUSIC   More self-discipline and practice are necessary, but Ike has a good sense of rhythm.

DRAMA   IKE ENJOYS BOTH TRAGEDY AND COMEDY AND IS A TALENTED CHARACTER ACTOR.

MATH   Ike has benefited from attending extra classes. He has definitely improved, but still makes faults through carelessness.

GEOGRAPHY   Ike's project on equatorial rain forests was very knowledgeable.

SCIENCE   Ike is uninterested in science and loses concentration easily. He also displays a tendency to talk. During practical work in the laboratory he meddles with the equipment. His techniques are very disappointing.

HISTORY   Ike has a thorough understanding of the Ancient World, especially of the lives of the Roman emperors. He has enjoyed learning about the gods and goddesses of Greek mythology.

ENGLISH   Although Ike makes little errors in his grammar, his creative writing is generally excellent. His descriptions are perceptive and often humorous. We have been grateful for his assistance in the library this year. As usual, Ike is top of the class at spelling.

Can you get *there*?

1 Look! **There's** Michelle!
2 Look at that, over **there**!
3 I know **they're** going away today.
4 **Their** house is huge.
5 I want one just like **theirs**.
6 **There's** been a dreadful accident.
7 Drop it! It's **theirs**.
8 **There's** been a snowfall overnight.
9 I liked **their** friends.
10 Have some more. **There's** plenty left.
11 I hate going **there**.
12 **They're** always arguing.

PUNCTUATION

CONTENTS

When you are writing, do you ever wonder if you need a comma (,) or an apostrophe ('), and where to put them? If so, you can find out more in this section of the book. These marks are part of punctuation. If you do all the puzzles in this section, good punctuation will become second nature. On the way, clear rules and tips will help you learn how to use each mark.

What is punctuation for?

Punctuation is a set of marks that you use in writing to divide up groups of words and make them easier to read.

When speaking, you vary the speed and loudness of words. In writing, punctuation shows these variations. It helps make the meaning clear because it shows how you would say the words, as well as where sentences begin, slow down and end.

See how the meaning changes depending on the punctuation you use:

Sam and Lucy, don't eat all that junk food!

Sam and Lucy don't eat all that junk food.

Without punctuation, even words that can only have one meaning are hard to read. Compare these letters, for instance:

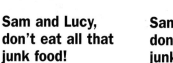

dear mrs peters
my dog lucky has disappeared i think i heard him barking inside your garage so i think he has gotten stuck in there i would really appreciate your help in finding my dog please call me or my dad when you get home
tina

Dear Mrs. Peters,
My dog Lucky has disappeared. I think I heard him barking inside your garage, so I think he has gotten stuck in there. I would really appreciate your help in finding my dog. Please call me or my Dad when you get home.
Tina

Punctuation is a vital writing skill. You need this skill to ensure that your writing is clear. It is also essential if you want to write more than very basic English.

Using this part of the book

This section looks at each punctuation mark in turn. Read through the guidelines, then test your punctuation skills by trying the puzzles which follow.

The book is not designed for writing in, so have some paper and a pen ready for your answers. You can check these at the back of the section.

Don't worry if you make mistakes. Work through the puzzles, then go back to anything you found hard.

You will come across a few grammatical terms, such as *subject, verb* etc. You can use the index on page 96 to find out where each term is explained.

How much punctuation?

SAM!!!!

In cartoon strips, you sometimes see lots of punctuation. This is because there is not enough room to explain the atmosphere and the characters' feelings. Extra punctuation is used instead.

Avoid using this much. Use enough for your meaning to be clear and no more. To show that someone said something in a particular way, describe how they said it, instead of relying on punctuation. For example: *"Sam!" he called angrily.*

The book explains the rules you must follow. Often, though, punctuation is up to you. In formal writing, like essays and letters to people you don't know well, keep close to the rules. If you are unsure, write short sentences. They are much easier to punctuate than long ones.

Punctuation summary

This shows you the different punctuation marks, each with its name and an example in which it is used. You will find out all about them as you work through this section of the book. Check that you can recognize them all, then do the puzzle below.

.	period	They have seen some shirts they want.	
,	comma	I like chicken, sausages and chocolate.	
:	colon	Here's what you must bring: a swimsuit, a towel and a sandwich.	
;	semicolon	The view is fine; the broken window is the problem.	
?	question mark	Who is that?	
!	exclamation point	That video is so stupid!	
'	apostrophe	Sarah's hat	
" "	quotation marks	He said, "Please wait for us by the fountain."	
( )	parentheses	Win a luxury vacation for two (details next week).	
-	hyphen	It must be a fast-spinning giant hat.	
–	dash	It is not a problem – just inconvenient.	
A B C	capital letters	At first, we found King Pong scary.	

Testing correspondence

How many of each of the following are there in this letter: periods, commas, colons, semicolons, exclamation points, hyphens, quotation marks, question marks and apostrophes?

The Select Residential Academy
Blimpton-on-Sea
September 3, 1995

Dear Mr. and Mrs. Fishplaite,
It is my sad duty to write to you regarding your daughter, Sonia, whom we must ask you to withdraw from S.R.A.
Sonia's attitude and manners have dramatically deteriorated; the poor quality of her work does nothing to compensate for this.
The events which prompted the decision are as follows: she locked her French teacher, Mademoiselle Ragou, in a cupboard and called her "an unenlightened stick insect". She later called me "a Komodo dragon" in front of all the girls and my staff at morning assembly!
We will of course help you in any way possible, and Sonia can remain here until the end of the semester. Would you like us to obtain a place for her at Highwall College, an establishment with the strong, disciplinarian approach which your daughter needs? I look forward to hearing from you in the very near future.
Yours sincerely,
K.D. Brittledge
Katrina Diana Brittledge
Headmistress

The period is the dot which you normally find at the end of a sentence. But it has several other uses too.

I just heard a cuckoo.

period

Ending a sentence

A sentence is a group of words that can stand on its own and make sense. It starts with a capital letter and must have a period at the end, unless you are using a question mark or an exclamation point (see below).

A period at the end of a sentence stands for a clear stop. It shows where, if you were speaking, your voice would drop and you would stop for a moment.

Here are the only two cases in which you do not use a full stop to end a sentence:

1 If a sentence is a question, it must end with a question mark, not a period. For example: *Which gate number do I go to?* This is explained on page 44.

2 If a sentence is about a strong feeling, you can end it with an exclamation point: I hate that! (See page 46.)

Sentence spotting

In order to know where to put periods, you have to be able to spot a sentence.

To qualify as a sentence, a group of words must make sense when it stands on its own. A typical sentence has a subject (a person or thing doing the action) and a verb (an action word): *The mailman opened the package.*

Sentences can be very short, though, and their meaning then depends on other sentences around them. Look at this example: *What did you say? Nothing.* Here, "nothing" is a sentence. If you know what was said before, it makes sense, and so it ends with a period.

Sentences can be linked with words like *and*, *but*, *so* or *because* to become one longer sentence, with a single period at the end. For example: *The mailman opened the package, and the counterfeit money fell out.*

Shortening words

You sometimes put a period at the end of an abbreviation (a short form of a word or expression). Here is a list of abbreviations which you should always end with a period:

1 Abbreviated titles. Examples: *Mr. Mrs. Dr. Rev.*
2 *Jr.* and *Sr.* These stand for *junior* and *senior*, and are often used with a name, as in *Bill Brogue, Jr.*
3 The initials (or first letters) of someone's name, as in *B. Brogue.*
4 The short form for *saint: St.*

In casual writing, other abbreviations often are written without periods, for instance USA instead of U.S.A. In both casual and formal writing, never use periods in abbreviations that people read out as if they were words. For example, UNICEF, which is always said *you-nee-seff*, is written without periods.

If an abbreviation is at the end of a sentence, use only one period: *His name is Bill Brogue, Jr.*

Pen problems

This message has six periods, but it also has black ink splodges that look like periods. Copy it out, keeping only the six correct periods.

I'll be home. late from school today, Mom. After volleyball practice, Miss. Mussly wants to discuss plans for our sports day. See you at about 6. p.m.. (Please. feed Misty as soon as you get in. Because of the kittens, I don't think. she should have to wait until 6.)

Costly dots

Freddy is trying to write a message. He must add three periods. Where should he put these to make his message as clear as possible?

SORRY I LET YOU DOWN IN INVERNESS I'LL EXPLAIN WHEN I SEE YOU MY WALLET WAS STILL IN YOUR BACKPACK WHEN YOU LEFT IN A HUFF PLEASE MEET ME FORT WILLIAM STATION ON SAT 8PM RIGHT OF LUGGAGE LOCKERS.

Pointless

Four of these pieces of writing are sentences that should end with a period. Decide which they are, and then write them out, ending each one with a period*.

1   Farther up the coast, the explorer
2   In Japan, cats have no tails
3   They were
4   All of a sudden, it vanished
5   They suffered dreadfully from cold, hunger
6   He cannot go into
7   It all seemed highly
8   She grabbed the mobile phone, lurched forward and
9   Sam looked blank
10 In front of her

Drifter's diary

This diary extract is written with no periods at all. Write it out, adding as many periods as possible and making sure that each sentence starts with a capital letter.

Monday

up at 11:00 am I didn't take a bath my sisters had left the bathroom in such a state that I didn't feel like it I went over to Jo Drone's Café for a hotdog because Dad was retiling the kitchen floor I just love that hot yellow mustard Teeny Tina came by for me later and we spent the whole afternoon at the DJ Club on my way home I bumped into my old classmate Sally Straite in Suburb Lane when I told her about how bored I felt, she told me to pull myself together and perhaps get a summer job she suggested I start by keeping a diary Sally thinks that the problems I have to iron out will soon become clear all I have to do is keep a diary for a few days and then read it through she reckons the problems will soon leap off the page at me

Sally's tel number is 666 3333 she said I can call her whenever I need some moral support I'm going to clean up the bathroom now then I'm going to take a bath and go to bed it's 10:00 pm

Dotty dramas

The police are investigating a train robbery. They have received some information from an anonymous witness, but it is difficult to make sense of, as there is not much punctuation. Split it up into sentences, using periods and capital letters.

I read the article in yesterday's Echo about the great pearl robbery I was on that train and am writing to let you know what I know there were hardly any passengers on the train in my carriage, there was only one man I noticed him because he had six briefcases and looked very nervous I soon dozed off all of a sudden, I woke up to the sound of terrible shouts a woman with a black mask over her face rushed toward me and threw a pile of shrimp and mayonnaise sandwiches in my face and all over my clothes then she climbed out of the window onto the platform the woman disappeared into the night while I started trying to clean off the

shrimp and mayonnaise at this point, I discovered there were lots of blue pearls mixed in with the food I scraped as much as I could into a plastic bag and got off the train nobody noticed me go in all the commotion now that I have read about what happened to the man with the briefcases, I want to hand in the pearls you can call me on 867 2382

* The hints on page 36 on how to spot a sentence will help you.

37

The comma stands for a short pause that separates a word or group of words from another in a sentence. You normally use it where you would pause very slightly if you were speaking. Commas are often essential to make the meaning clear.

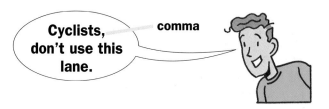

Cyclists, don't use this lane.

comma

·*Cyclists don't use this lane* has another meaning from the sentence above.

Commas in lists

When you list words in a sentence, use commas to separate them. Normally, if the last two parts of the list are joined with *and*, you don't put a comma in front of *and*. For example: *These are made from eggs, flour, water, cheese and herbs.*

Sometimes, though, you need a comma in front of *and*, to make sure the sentence is clear: *Jim ordered tomato soup, cheese, and coffee ice cream.* The comma makes clear that he did not order *cheese and coffee ice cream*!

When you list adjectives (describing words) before a noun (a naming word), commas between the adjectives are not always needed. In *deep, cold pond*, the comma sounds best. In *big blue eyes*, it is unnecessary. Put commas in when it would be natural to pause*.

Long sentences

To know where commas go in long sentences, it helps to know how sentences are made. A typical one has at least one main clause (this has a subject and a verb, makes sense on its own, and could itself be a sentence). It may also have 1) a subordinate clause – this too has a verb, but depends on a main clause for its meaning; 2) a phrase – this adds meaning; it is often short and says where, when or how something happens.

phrase

main clause (she = subject; handed = verb)

All of a sudden, she handed me my passport, which was now torn and dirty.

subordinate clause (was = verb)

Comma or no comma?

Here are some rules and guidelines on when to use commas in long sentences:

1 Put a comma before *and, but, or, nor, for* and *yet* when they join independent clauses, unless the clauses are very short. For example: *We went to the fair, and my pig won a prize. You go and I'll follow.*

2 Use a comma to separate off a phrase at the start of a sentence: *After this fight, they felt better.* After a short phrase, the comma is optional.

If the phrase comes later, you may need commas on either side of it in order to make the meaning clear: *She whistled and luckily her dog followed* (commas are optional). *She whistled and, after a tiff with a passing cat, her dog followed* (commas here are best).

3 Commas may be needed to separate a subordinate clause from a main clause. If the subordinate clause is first, a comma is usual: *While Zoe wrote, Pip washed up.*

4 For a subordinate clause starting with *who, whom* or *which*, a comma must separate it off if it is not essential to the meaning. Leaving out the comma makes the clause a more important part of the sentence, and so may change its meaning. For example:

He threw away the eggs, which were broken.

He threw away the eggs which were broken.

38   *The comma can affect the meaning: compare *a pretty small girl* (quite small) with *a pretty, small girl* (pretty and small).

Two by two

For each pair of pictures below, there are two sentences. Match each sentence with the correct picture.

The apples, which were red, had worms in them.

The apples which were red had worms in them.

The boys, who were wearing red, all had black hair.

The boys who were wearing red all had black hair.

The ham, which was cold, came with salad.

The ham which was cold came with salad.

A comma or two

Copy out these sentences, adding one comma each to sentences 1 - 4, and two commas each to sentences 5 - 9.

1   **My brother is lazy rude and arrogant.**
2   **Many people will read this story although it is very badly written.**
3   **Stefie has brought flowers ice cream and chocolates.**
4   **Meanwhile Susie was cycling home.**
5   **I took the books which were old torn and shabby but left the good ones for my mother.**
6   **The three bands that were playing were Sound and Emotion Billy and the Cheesemakers and the Blue Moon Band.**
7   **He waved at Lisa who was watching from the window and walked down the street.**
8   **The rugby players who were exhausted limped off the field together.**

Lily's list

Lily has written out her shopping list without putting any commas in. Can you add 14 commas?

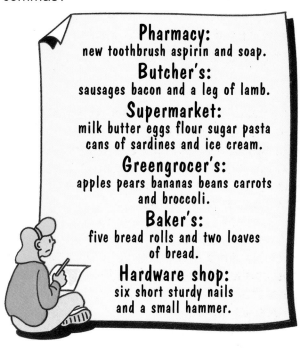

Pharmacy:
new toothbrush aspirin and soap.
Butcher's:
sausages bacon and a leg of lamb.
Supermarket:
milk butter eggs flour sugar pasta cans of sardines and ice cream.
Greengrocer's:
apples pears bananas beans carrots and broccoli.
Baker's:
five bread rolls and two loaves of bread.
Hardware shop:
six short sturdy nails and a small hammer.

Comma commotion

There are too many commas in this clipping from a catalog. Rewrite the descriptions, taking out 11 commas that should not be there.

These Cosifit earmuffs are warm, comfortable, and suitable for anyone from 6 to 60! The adjustable head strap means that however, big or small your head may be, Cosifit earmuffs, will always fit!

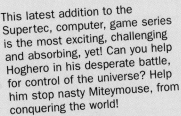

This latest addition to the Supertec, computer, game series is the most exciting, challenging and absorbing, yet! Can you help Hoghero in his desperate battle, for control of the universe? Help him stop nasty Miteymouse, from conquering the world!

Every trendy, teenager needs a Staralarm! When you go to bed, just set the alarm by choosing a time and a voice - the voice of your favorite, pop star. What better way to wake up than to the sound of Kool Malone, Freddy, and the Freezers, or Ritchy Roon?

39

Ellipsis

You use three periods in a row (...) to show that some words are missing from a sentence or to show that a sentence is unfinished.

I must not get these shoes...

Tinker, tailor, soldier... beggarman, thief.

You should not use an ellipsis after expressions such as *and so on* and *et cetera*. People sometimes do, but a single period here is correct.

Comma tips

Page 38 explains how to use commas*. Sometimes, though, it is hard to decide where to put them. Here are two tips:

1 Make sure each complete sentence ends with a period, then try reading aloud, listening for natural pauses. For each pause, think whether a comma is needed.
2 If you still do not know where to put the commas, perhaps your sentence is too complicated or too long, and needs to be rewritten.

Numbers

In math, the period is used as the decimal point (as in *1.5* to mean *one and a half*). Always write the decimal point very clearly, as the difference between, for example, 1.5 and 15 is enormous.

In most written English, the comma is used to break up numbers that are over four figures long, for example, 10,000. You start from the right and put a comma in after each set of three numerals. This helps to make it easier to read long numbers. You do not normally do this in math and science.

Look at this example: *Mrs. Fern, the head of my old school and the piano teacher who, years ago, gave my brother lessons, left to go to work in a circus.*

In order to say that Mrs. Fern, who is a former headmistress and piano teacher, went to work in a circus, you must rewrite the sentence. Because too many details are attached to the main information, the sentence could mean that Mrs. Fern, the headmistress and the former piano teacher (three different people)

went to work in a circus. A comma before *and the teacher* will not help.

Here is a possible rewrite: *Mrs. Fern, who was the headmistress of my old school and was also the piano teacher who, years ago, gave my brother lessons, left to go to work in a circus.*

To do the puzzles on these two pages, you may need to look back at pages 35 and 37.

Mix and match

Here are eight sentences, each cut in two. By looking at the capital letters, periods and commas, see if you can match up the sixteen pieces to make the eight most suitable sentences.

, then grudgingly guided them down the dark alley.

but I still could not make up my mind.

I thought it over

In the late afternoon,

After the detective's visit

, which is in Canada.

Andy and his parents have moved to Gap,

and quickly decided on a course of action.

The woman looked down her nose at them,

I decided to go to the police station.

He gave me some sound advice,

which is in France.

, no longer felt in the mood to work.

The man wrinkled up his nose in disdain

Jan and her family have moved to Arcola

but agreed to show them the documents.

*Commas are also used in letter writing (see page 56) and in direct speech, such as *I said, "Come back!"* (see page 52).

Stop gap

Copy out these periods, using five periods, eleven commas and an ellipsis (...) to complete them.

1 **Live coverage of this fascinating sporting event will begin on Radio Livewire at 6**

2 **There were 18000 people at the concert so our chances of bumping into Gemma Jim and Sam were very slight**

3 **Disheartened the explorers began their return journey setting off**

4 **In early Roman times theaters were built of wood**

5 **At last wet gasping and exhausted they reached the bus shelter**

6 **The sun which we had not seen for two months blinded us**

Printer problems

This printer prints an ellipsis wherever a period or a comma is needed, as well as where an ellipsis is correct. Copy the text, replacing the ellipses with periods and commas wherever you think would be best.

Tennessee Open Zoo Wild Cats Leaflet

Nearly all wild cats live in rainforests... They hunt and eat meat... They have very good eyesight... and often...

(Cathy... please research all the general points for the above opening paragraph... When you have done so... write them up on my computer... The file name is WCL...)

The tiger is the largest cat... It is extremely strong... It hunts for its food... catching large animals if it can... Rather than go hungry... though... it eats small creatures such as frogs... ants... worms... beetles and so on...

(Cathy... please also research and write the section on leopards... I have gathered the relevant books... folders... cuttings... etc... You will find them all on my desk... to the left of the pile of parrot leaflets...)

Hasty homework

This essay has periods and capital letters, but no other punctuation. Copy it, adding commas where needed (the photos may help you).

<u>My summer vacation</u>

For my summer vacation I went to Agadir a beach paradise in Morocco. I stayed in a luxury hotel with three enormous swimming pools a movie theater two dance clubs a jogging track and a computer games room.

The hotel is by a beautiful long white beach and the bedrooms which have balconies overlook the sea. My Mom and Dad had a hard time getting to sleep because of the waves crashing down below. My room which had no balcony and was just around the corner was quiet.

I did not like the pools as much as the sea although they did have lots of truly awesome water rapids waves and whirlpools. The two swimming pools which have lots of sun loungers around them are always crowded. Because the third one has lanes in it for serious swimming it is usually empty. On the beach there were huge waves which I loved. One morning after a storm I saw some jellyfish on the beach.

The food was wonderful. The hotel has chefs from all over the world so we mostly ate Chinese food and Moroccan food which were our favorites.

Even though we only spent a day there our visit to Marrakesh was the highlight of the whole vacation. It is a really exciting town and the markets and tiny ancient streets are full of weird things like carpets olives and spices all piled up leather bags and sandals.

Because it was spring and the weather was not too hot I really enjoyed this vacation.

colon

Make sure you pack the following items: map, compass, flashlight, whistle and waterproof jacket.

semicolon

Rehearsing this piece of music is fun; performing it in front of people is the problem.

The colon is two dots, one above the other. The semicolon is made of a dot over a comma. Both of them represent a pause in a sentence (a longer pause than shown by a comma and a shorter one than shown by a period). They are not followed by a capital letter.

The semicolon

This has two main uses:

1 It can separate two closely linked main clauses* of similar importance. It is used instead of a period or a word like *and* or *but*. For example: *He lifted the lid; the lost gems fell out.*

In this example, the semicolon gives a dramatic effect of short, linked pieces. Using a period instead, the effect is jerky: *He lifted the lid. The lost gems fell out.* With *and*, it is less dramatic: *He lifted the lid and the lost gems fell out.*

When you link two main clauses with words like *but, then* or *even so*, put a semicolon in front of the link word if there is a comma in either clause. For example: *Their train was late; even so, they made the connection.*

2 The semicolon is also used to break up the different items in a list.

Normally, you use commas for this (see page 38). But if the items in the list are long and complicated (which often means they need commas themselves), you use semicolons instead. For example: *To make this bag, you will need a large, sturdy needle for sewing tough fabrics; extremely thick thread made of nylon or some sort of synthetic material; coarse, durable gray fabric with the logo printed on it; and finally, a white button of any kind**.*

The colon

The colon does two things:

1 It can introduce a list of items. For example: *To build a model train tunnel, you will need: a shoe box, sandpaper, paints and glue.* You can also write a list with no colon (*...you will need a shoe box, sandpaper...*). By drawing attention to the start of the list, the colon helps to make the writing clear.

In two cases, the colon is essential:
a) when the list is laid out as a column.
You will need:
a shoe box
sandpaper
paints
glue.

b) when the list begins *You will need the following*: or *Here is a checklist of things you should do*: or expressions like this. In cases like these, you can tell that you need a colon before the start of the list itself because you cannot continue to read without a pause.

2 The colon can go between two main clauses to introduce an explanation or a summary of the first clause:
We soon solved the mystery of the missing chops: Rover had eaten them. (explanation)
She read the letter and gave a huge grin: the news was good. (summary)
You also use a colon after *Dear...* at the start of a formal letter (see page 56), and when you write the time: *6:15 a.m.*

*This is the part of a sentence that contains a subject and a verb, and which makes sense on its own.
**Here a semicolon is used before *and finally*, but a comma would be possible instead.

Fishy prizes

Here are the three winning entries in a cooking contest. To make the recipes clear, where in each one should you add two colons, a comma and a semicolon?

First Prize

Quiche Marine – For the pastry, you will need flour, butter or margarine, one egg.

For the filling, have ready the following fresh shrimp, shelled; crab meat either fresh or from a can cream, eggs and seasoning.

Make the pastry in the usual way, roll it out and line a flan dish with it. Mix the ingredients for the filling, pour them onto the pastry and bake for 25 minutes.

Second Prize

Perfect Fish Pie – To make the potato layer, mix together some mashed potatoes, milk and eggs.

For the fish layer, get the following mixture ready: chopped fresh flounder, sole and salmon in equal quantities. Mix these together, adding a dash of salt and a squeeze of lemon juice.

The ingredients for the cheese sauce are equal amounts of milk, cream and yogurt; a tablespoon of flour; finely grated cheddar cheese; two beaten egg yolks. Stir these together in a pan, heating gently until thick. Don't include the cheese this must go in after the sauce has thickened and is off the heat.

To assemble the pie do the following: put half the potato in the bottom of an ovenproof dish; place the fish mixture on top, making sure it is well spread over all the potato; cover with the remaining potato finally, pour the cheese sauce over the top and bake for 30 minutes. Serve with a green salad.

Young Chef of the Month

A prize for entries from cooks aged 11 or under.

Green Fishcakes with Pink Sauce – For the fishcakes, mash together these ingredients poached cod, boiled potatoes and two raw eggs. Add a mixture of finely chopped fresh herbs. Include parsley and chives, and one of the following dill, fennel, sorrel. Also add a knob of butter. Shape this mixture into fishcakes and fry gently in a little butter and corn oil.

For the sauce mince some peeled shrimp and mix with lots of sour cream.

When the fishcakes are ready, heat the sauce and pour it into the plates. Place the fishcakes on top of the sauce. As a main course, serve with boiled new potatoes and broccoli as a snack, serve with crusty bread.

Getting it right

Copy out these ads, adding either a colon or a semicolon to each.

Washomatic for sale. This machine is a genuine bargain: it is only 12 years old; there is not a single visible patch of rust on it last but not least, it does not leak. Phone Johnny on 324 5543.

Attention, old pen collectors! Green Silhouette pen for sale, 1952 model. Features included original case, gold nib, embossed logo. Phone Pipa Pentop, 324 5682.

For sale or rent, garage in Bach Alley. Contact Mrs. Lucas, 3 Bach Square.

WANTED YOUNG PERSON TO DELIVER NEWSPAPERS IN COMBE PARK AREA. MUST HAVE OWN BIKE. APPLY TO NAT'S NEWS.

Gardener sought. The following qualifications are required familiarity with Supermow, sound knowledge of organic vegetable growing and garden pest control. Phone 324-3344.

Hair excesses

Copy out these pieces of writing, taking out the surplus punctuation. Each one has an unnecessary colon or semicolon.

Come to us: for a wide range of hair care: perms, hair straightening, coloring, highlighting, beading, hair extensions.

Our perms are perfect in every way: gentle, lasting; and adapted to suit your face shape.

Choose between three wonderful shampoos: frosted yogurt and banana for dry hair; lemon and lime cocktail for oily hair; finally, for problem hair, mango and chili revitalizing magic; or Brazil nut balsam.

Always follow up a shampoo with a good conditioner: this guarantees good hair condition. Among our dozens of choices, we recommend either: deep action strawberry, marigold petal extract or luxury oatmilk.

Treat yourself to: a head massage, the ideal treatment for tired heads. You get a 15 minute massage given by an expert; generous amounts of the best massage oils; a shampoo and blow dry.

We give you the hairdo you want. Once you have it you will want to keep it; to help you, we stock 30 varieties of hair spray. Also in stock: hundreds of mousses, hair gels; and styling spritzes.

43

The question mark is a sign that goes on the end of a sentence which asks a question. It shows where, in speech, you would raise your voice a little, then pause as for a period.

Can you hear me?

question mark

Direct questions

The kind of question which ends with a question mark is called a direct question. It is a question to which an answer is expected. This is how typical direct questions look:

They begin with a capital letter.

*Are you tired?**

first word is a verb or a question word (see right)

subject comes after the verb

Why are you tired?

They end with a question mark.

Longer questions may begin with extra words, but the order (verb/subject or question word/verb/subject) is the same. For example: *So then, why are you tired?*

Direct questions can be very short and have no verb or subject. For example: *Why?*

As the question mark is used instead of a period, you put a capital letter after it: *Why are you tired? It is only ten.*

Indirect questions

An indirect question is a type of sentence which looks a little like a direct question but is a normal sentence. It ends with a period, not a question mark. Here is an example: *She is asking if you can hear.*

It is a sentence which tells you about a question that was asked. You can think of it as a reported question.

To spot an indirect question, look for expressions like *ask* or *wonder* used with *if, whether* or a question word (see above right). Notice too that the word order is subject/verb (*you can*), not the other way around (*can you*) as for a direct question.

Question words

Here are the most commonly used question words:

Whose?
Whom? Where? Why?
What? Who?
When? Which?
How?

Some of these words are not used only in questions. They can double up as other kinds of words. For example: *When I was on the ferry, I felt sick.*

Question tags

Question tags are short and are tagged onto the end of a statement, after a comma: *You play the violin, don't you?* These question tags belong to spoken English, so avoid them in formal writing such as essays. However, if you write one, remember that it turns the sentence into a question, so put a question mark on the end.

——Ask a straight question——

How many of the following are direct questions that need a question mark, and how many are indirect ones that don't?

1 I asked her if she could bring him to my party
2 Can you bring your brother to my party
3 Does anyone know where I put my watch
4 Is there a candy store around here
5 Did you ask if there is a candy store around here
6 When do you think you will be able to help out on the school newspaper
7 Will you be able to help out on the school newspaper
8 Who do you feel we could invite along

44 *In very informal, spoken English, questions are sometimes made without moving the verb: *You're tired?* If you write down a question like this, for example in a note, put a question mark on the end.

Awkward questions

Each of the ten questions on this police report have been printed in jumbled order. Can you figure out what the questions might be? (They are all direct questions.)

1   live you here Do?

2   night were eleven Where at o'clock last you?

3   with who TV are of friends were What watching the the you names four ?

4   unusual Did your you friends or of anything hear one?

5   you friend a Jack have Do named?

6   night here Was last he?

7   heard around you who the Gang, gang the Have a of of hang Burly thugs neighborhood?

8   their them you to leader or Jack ever about Hasn't boasted mentioned being?

9   heard unusual if asked when Why lie I you you you had anything did?

10 so it Was Jack you he parents' night who could gave your garage key to hide there the last?

Searching questions

Help Jan enter a songwriting competition. Copy the lyrics she has written, adding periods or question marks to the ends of the seven lines that need them.

One day, you'll leave, won't you
When I asked you last summer,
You said you'd be true,
But now, I just wonder

Why is it always me
That gets left behind
In this state, I can't see
How life can ever be kind

Friends are no better
Why are they never around
When I need a shoulder
Oh, when will I stop feeling so blue

Questionnaire mix-up

Sam has written a list of questions which form a character questionnaire. They run on, one after the other, but have gotten mixed up with other, incorrectly punctuated pieces. Can you pick the right line, from each batch of three, to follow from the previous one?

1   a) How old are

2   a) the boys in the team. How would you describe
    b) you? How would you describe
    c) your two sisters, would you describe

3   a) yourself? Are you
    b) yourself and your sister. Are you
    c) your best friend. Is she

4   a) generous or selfish. I wonder whether you feel
    b) mean and difficult, We wonder if you like
    c) lively or quiet? We wonder if you like

5   a) jeans or skirts best. Are
    b) red or pink nail polish best? Are
    c) country and western music? Are

6   a) your eyes blue
    b) you short or tall.
    c) your eyes dark or light.

7   a) green or hazel? Can you
    b) , green or hazel? Can you
    c) green or hazel. Can you

8   a) tell me how how often you play tennis. Do you like
    b) ride a bike. Do you enjoy
    c) swim, play tennis and ride a bike? You enjoy

9   a) playing the piano, don't you? Do you prefer
    b) playing the piano, don't you... Do you prefer
    c) playing the piano? Do you prefer

10 a) sports to quiet things like reading.
    b) playing computer games or watching TV?
    c) playing computer, games or watching TV?

45

I'm scared!

exclamation point

The exclamation point is a vertical line over a dot. It can go on the end of a sentence instead of a period. An exclamation point shows that the sentence expresses a strong feeling such as anger, delight, surprise or fear.

When do you use one?

Exclamation points are optional. You can always end the type of sentence described above with a period.

There is no rule about this. The best advice is to use few exclamation points. If you use too many, they have less effect. Use one on the end of short expressions (such as *Ouch!*), and where you want to draw attention to the strength of feeling.

Look at this example: *What a storm! It was unbelievable! The thunder and lightning were continuous, the sky was black and the rain came down in torrents! Within seconds, we were soaked! I have never been so scared!*

With fewer exclamation points, the effect is stronger: *What a storm! It was unbelievable. The thunder and lightning were continuous, the sky was black and the rain came down in torrents. Within seconds, we were soaked. I have never been so scared.*

Where you place exclamation points changes the meaning slightly by drawing attention to the sentences that have them. In this piece of writing, you could underline the scary effect of the storm by putting one on the end: *I have never been so scared!*

Short expressions

A tip for dealing with more than one expression of surprise, anger and so on is to use a mixture of commas and exclamation marks. For example, you should avoid writing *Wow! How brilliant!* Instead, write *Wow, how brilliant!*

It can also go on the end of an order or a short expression to show that they are said loudly or with lots of feeling:

Ouch!

What a dumb thing to do!

Call the police!

Remember, as the exclamation point is used instead of a period, it is followed by a capital letter.

One only

Where you want an exclamation mark, one is always enough. You may see two or three used, but you should only use one.

Overkill

Copy this newspaper article, cutting eight exclamation points and replacing two of these with commas. (Adjust capital letters as necessary.)

What a calamity!!! Dire is to lose its railway station bathroom unless urgent action is taken. This, at least, is what the Association of Dire Residents (ADR) fear, following their meeting with the Station's Passenger Liaison Committee (SPLC) yesterday.

According to the ADR spokesperson, Gail Bigwail, the Committee is intent on cutting costs. Losing the toilet will save exactly the amount they are looking for.

What an unnecessary, backward step!! The shortest journey from Dire is 23 minutes, and with no bathroom at Dire Central, passengers would just have to keep their legs crossed!!!

We agree with Ivor Right, also of the ADR, who points out that, with a little thought and care, small savings could be made here and there, thus allowing the bathroom to be kept open. How true, Mr. Right, and how eagerly we will publicize your views! The ADR is planning a Day of Action in the near future. So cheer up, Citizens of Dire! Buy the Dire Echo every day! And we will keep you informed!!

Surprise, surprise

Dawn has come top in her class. Her little brother took all the messages she received and scratched out some of the punctuation. Each message should have an extra exclamation point, comma and period. Copy the four messages, adding the right punctuation in each of the scratched spaces.

Foxes' Dale
Boarding School for Boys

Wow, you do have a brain after all ⚡
I suppose I'm impressed ⚡ though it's pretty horrible having to ⚡ admit it
See you on Saturday, Einstein.
Charlie

Great stuff, Miss Brainypants⚡After Lady Banstead's stunning announcement ⚡I can only beg to remain your proud best friend⚡
See you at volleyball, clever socks!
Di

Wan Girls' School

Congratulations ⚡ Dawn ⚡ The whole school is proud of you ⚡ Best wishes for next year,
Helga Banstead
(Headmistress)

Florida Keys Hotel

Dear Dawn,
You brilliant girl⚡I just can't get over how clever you are⚡and I'm dying to get home from this wretched business trip so I can give you the hug you deserve⚡
Watch your brothers. Charlie will be green with envy but OK. Jamie will hate you getting all the attention!
See you on Saturday.
Lots of love,
Mom

Slot machine roundup

This puzzle gives you a chance to test yourself on all the punctuation explained so far in this book (from page 35 to here).

Someone has played on the fruit machine and jumbled the last two parts of each sentence. Copy the first pieces, then figure out which center piece and which end piece match up with it. (Look closely at the punctuation.)

First piece	Center piece	End piece
Toward the end of the meal	000 times more money than	he paid us last summer.
Toward the end of the meal	they had decided to go home or	their boat will dock in Singapore.
We asked them if	times more than	that!
I wonder	a chest full of coins, but they should be covered with old toys; a rusty anchor on a chain	without having a desert.
When	, the waiter got so slow we had to leave	didn't it?
To put on the show, we asked for four props	the café really did get very full,	if they had gone to the club.
This is what we need for the photograph	does he think	and a bucket.
How dreadful, we need 10,	if he thinks	their boat will dock in Singapore?
The current rate for grape picking is 10	: a pair of stilts, a clown's outfit, an overcoat	; a flag with a skull and crossbones.

The apostrophe looks like a comma, but it goes higher on the line. The top of it lines up with the tops of letters like *l* and *k*.

apostrophe

Annie's cat is at the door.

Two uses

The apostrophe is used in two ways:
1 It can show that some letters are missing (as in *The cat's at the door*, where *cat's* stands for *cat is*). This is explained on page 50.
2 It can also show possession (who something belongs to), as in the example, *Annie's cat*.

's for possession

To show who something belongs to, you normally add *'s* to the owner's name. Here are some examples of this possessive *'s*:

Fred's shirt (the shirt that belongs to Fred, or the shirt of Fred)

the teacher's car (the car that belongs to the teacher, or the car of the teacher)

King Midas's gold (the gold belonging to King Midas, or the gold of King Midas)

the actress's wig (the wig belonging to the actress, or the wig of the actress)

This *'s* is correct for all nouns (naming words) when they are singular. Singular means there is only one, as opposed to plural (more than one). For example, *car* is singular (only one), and *cars* is plural (more than one). Look at the examples above and notice that even singular nouns which end in *s* add *'s*.

Plural nouns

Most nouns have an extra *s* on the end when they are plural (more than one). For example: *parents*. To show possession for these, you add only an apostrophe*. Here are some examples:
my parents' car (the car that belongs to my parents)
the Smiths' car (the car that belongs to the Smiths)

Unusual plurals

A few nouns do not have an extra *s* or *es* when they are plural, but change in another way. For example: *child, children*. To show possession for these, add *'s*. For example: *the children's room*.

Spotting possessives

To tell if a noun with an *s* needs an apostrophe, try using *of*. For example, for *Annie's cat*, you can say the *cat of Annie*. This means it is possessive and needs *'s*.

Filling the gap

For these sentences, which word shown in blue fits the gap?

1 **His ... house is in Armadillo.**
parents'/parents
2 **Their ... bedrooms are all in the attic.**
children's/childrens'
3 **We ended up in the ... worst diner.**
towns/town's/towns'
4 **My ... colors are scarlet, blue and yellow.**
teams/teams'/team's
5 **My favorite ... annual tour starts next week.**
bands/band's/bands'
6 **Mrs. ... next-door neighbor is a retired filmstar.**
Jones/Jones's
7 **Of this ... two radios, only one is working.**
ship's/ships'/ships's
8 **The conductor would not let us onto the ... top deck.**
buses'/bus's
9 **By the end of the match, the 13 ... energy had completely run out.**
player's/players'/players
10 **The ... garage had been emptied overnight.**
Brown's/Browns'

*For nouns which end in *ch, sh, s, x* or *z*, and a few which end in *o*, add *es*. For some of those ending in *y*, the *y* changes to *i* and you add *es*. For example: *bush, bushes; baby, babies.*

Get the facts right

Look at the words and pictures below. For the first set, the correct phrase is *the cats' basket*. Add apostrophes to make the remaining eleven phrases. Make sure that the nouns in your phrases change to plural where necessary to match the pictures.

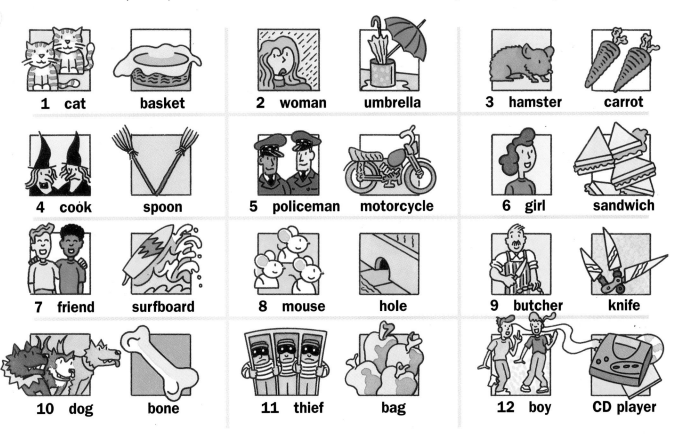

1 cat   basket

2 woman   umbrella

3 hamster   carrot

4 cook   spoon

5 policeman   motorcycle

6 girl   sandwich

7 friend   surfboard

8 mouse   hole

9 butcher   knife

10 dog   bone

11 thief   bag

12 boy   CD player

Photo album

Of the two sentences given for each photo, only one matches the picture. Can you work out which?

A1 My cousins' hair is jet black.
A2 My cousin's hair is jet black.

B1 The girl's room is blue.
B2 The girls' room is blue.

C1 My uncles' vans are purple.
C2 My uncle's vans are purple.

D1 All the baby's clothes are striped.
D2 All the babies' clothes are striped.

E1 My aunt's eyes are green.
E2 My aunts' eyes are green.

F1 Their dogs' bowls are yellow.
F2 Their dog's bowls are yellow.

49

More about apostrophes

Contractions

Page 48 explains how you use apostrophes to show who owns something (as in *Annie's cat*). Apostrophes are also used to show where there is a contraction. A contraction is when some letters are missing in a word because it is said in a shortened form. In the examples on the right, *cat's* and *can't* are contractions. They are short for *cat is* and *cannot*.

Her cat's at the door.

I can't see it.

Common ones

Most contractions are short forms of verbs. Here are some examples:
'm short for *am* (as in *I'm a gym teacher*);
's short for *is* (as in *He's a math teacher*), or short for *has* (as in *She's left*).

Contractions are also often short forms of a verb used with *not*. For example, *isn't* is short for *is not* (*She isn't here*).

Avoiding them

Contractions are part of spoken English. Never use them in essays and written homework, nor in formal writing (letters asking for information or work, for example). You can use them in written English if you are writing something informal like a message or letter to a friend, or when you are writing down what someone said.

Unusual ones

A few expressions, such as *o'clock*, are contractions which are always written with an apostrophe. This is because the full expression is out of date and is no longer used. *O'clock* stands for *of the clock*.

A few family names are also written with an apostrophe. For example: *O'Connor*.

Trouble shooting

People often make mistakes with apostrophes. To help you to avoid this, here is a summary of what you need to know.

1 To show possession:
• for singular nouns, add *'s*.
Example: the *teacher's pet*;
• for plural nouns that end in *s*, add an apostrophe after the *s*.
Example: *the three teachers' pet* (the pet of the three teachers);
• for plural nouns that do not end in *s*, add *'s* (as for singular nouns).
Example: *the children's room*.
• Expressions such as *baker's, doctor's* and *at Jessie's* are possessives. They are short for *baker's shop, doctor's surgery, at Jessie's house*, and so on. You must write them with *'s* on the end.

2 Use an apostrophe to show a contraction (words with letters missing, such as *I'd**). Examples are *I'd* (for *I had, I should* or *I would*), *won't* (for *will not*), *can't* (for *cannot*), *you've* (for *you have*), *she's* (for *she has*) and *don't* (for *do not*). Contractions are common in spoken English. Avoid them when writing, except in informal writing.

3 Do not confuse *its* and *it's*:
• *its* means "belonging to it", as in *Look at the bike! Its saddle is broken*. In this sense, *its* does not have an apostrophe;
• *it's* is the contraction of *it is*.

If you are in any doubt, try putting *it is* where you are having the problem. If the sentence makes sense, *it's* is right. If not, try *his* (or *her*). If the sentence now makes sense, then *its* is correct. For example, in *Its saddle is broken*, you cannot replace *its* by *it is*, but *His saddle is broken* makes sense, so *its* is correct.

——— Itsy-bitsy ———

Fill the gaps in this description with either *it, its* or *it's*.

Like all spiders, ...it has eight legs. ... overall length is about that of a human hand. The web ...makes out of ... own silk is so strong that even small animals get trapped in .... not able to eat solid food, so ... fills ... prey with special juices to turn ... into liquid ... can eat.

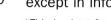

50

*This is short for *I had, I should* or *I would*.

Chatterbox contractions

These speech bubbles each contain one or more contractions (words with letters missing). Rewrite the words in full without the contractions.

> **Maria's paintbrushes aren't in the same box as yours.**

> **The baker's is closed and the supermarket doesn't sell Mr. Duff's doughnuts.**

> **It's not worth mending my tennis racket: all its strings are broken and the handle's cracked.**

> **I won't be allowed to come unless you'll give me a lift home.**

> **There's nothing on that they'd really like to see.**

> **Its streets are so quiet and dull, especially when it's raining.**

> **I'd rather go to Suzie's, if she's home.**

> **They'd all gone by the time we got there.**

> **That baker's a surly man.**

> **They've gone to the doctor's.**

Filling apostrophes

There are eleven apostrophes missing in this message. Copy it out and add them in.

> **Is going to the dentists a nightmare for your child? Come to us. Were the childrens specialists. Some dentists terrify kiddies. Its their approach thats all wrong. Ours is sensitive and fun. Our offices look like kids playrooms, but theyre equipped with the latest technology so everythings as quick, painless and easy as possible - even fillings are fun here. Theres constant music and we tell the kids spooky or fun stories while we work. Well take good care of your childrens health and looks without giving cause for fear and tears!**

Crime busters

Read Sergeant Jones's notes on the suspected burglary at the Harrises' bungalow. Decide which word or expression from the red list below fits each gap. (Use each one once only.)

Mr and Mrs 1 are away on business. The 2 daughter got home from school at six. As soon as she put her 3 in the 4 front door, she knew something was wrong. One of the 5 glass panels was cracked. A brave girl, she walked in.

Everything appeared normal except that all the inside 6 were open, whereas some are usually kept closed, and her 7 dogs weren't barking. The 8 behavior was odd and they seemed groggy. "9 very unusual. 10 always waiting by the door because 11 want to go out." She thinks the 12 had been doped.

Other strange things were that the garage 13 usual hiding place had been searched, a camera was missing from her 14 wardrobe, and in the study, the computer was on and the message on 15 screen said: "Now 16 time to reveal the truth." The Harrises' daughter said her 17 will be back tonight.

Before leaving, I checked the other 18 and all the windows, which all looked fine. The other 19 on the street had not been disturbed.

Harrises' / door's / doors / bungalow's / parents' / dogs' / it's / It's / doors / They're / key / dogs / they / Harris / bungalows / its / parents' / key's / parents

When you write the words that someone said, you use quotation marks to show where their words begin and end*. The opening marks look like two upside down apostrophes. The closing ones look like two apostrophes. Quotation marks are also quite often called quotes.

John said, "They've quotation found the way out." marks

Direct speech

Direct speech is when you write spoken words in quotation marks. The words go inside the quotation marks with their punctuation, though you sometimes have to adjust the punctuation a little.

The verb that introduces the spoken words (*say, ask, whisper* and so on) can go first, last, or in the middle. Here you can see how the punctuation should be in each case:

1 If the verb is first:

> two capital letters: one at the start of the sentence, and one where the spoken words start

He said, "They've found the way out."

> comma** at the end of the introduction, before "

> period before "

2 If the verb is last:

> one capital letter only

"They've found the way out," he said.

> comma after the spoken words, before " (replacing the period that the spoken words ended with)

3 If the verb is in the middle:

> comma within the quotation marks

"From what I can see," he said, peering into the binoculars, "they've found the way out."

> comma before "

> one period at the end, before "

Think of the words in quotation marks and the words that introduce them as a sentence. Whichever of the three patterns you follow, the sentence starts with a capital letter and ends with a full stop (or *?* or *!*). If the closing quotation marks are on the end (as in 1 and 3), the full stop (or *?* or *!*) is within them.

Ending with ? and !

If the spoken words end with a question mark or exclamation point, this is what you do:
He asked, "Have you found the way out?"
He said, "They've found the way out!"

> *?* or *!* before " (no need for a period)

"Have you found the way out?" he asked.
"They've found the way out!" he said.

> no capital letter after *?* or *!* (notice that this breaks the usual rule about having a capital letter after *!* and *?*)

Dialogue

When you write a dialogue (two or more people's spoken words), you can start a new paragraph (see page 56) each time you switch to a new speaker. This helps to make clear who is speaking:
"Who did you say?" she asked.
"I said Fred, but I meant Ted!" he answered, laughing.

Indirect quotes

There is another way of writing people's words, called indirect quotes. This is when you report the words that someone said, rather than giving their exact spoken words. For example: *John said that they had found the way out.* In indirect quotes, you never use quotation marks.

*A colon is sometimes used here instead of the comma: *He said: "They've found the way out."*
**A colon is sometimes used here instead of the comma: *He said: "They've found the way out."*

What was that?

Write what these six people are saying, using direct quotes. For each one, start with *he* or *she said* (or *he* or *she asked*, in the case of questions). Then do the same again, but put *he/she said* or *he/she asked* at the end. Try to get all the punctuation right.

> **Right, put your pens down now, please!**

> **Carol's taken my pen.**

> **Jamie was copying Tracy's answers.**

> **I can't believe how hard that was!**

> **Did you hear about Ros and Kate?**

> **I've left my lunch box at home!**

Adventure diary

In total, there are 12 sets of quotation marks missing from these diary entries. Read them through, then copy out all the sections that need quotation marks, adding these in (and adjusting the punctuation to go with them).

Great Rocks Vacation Center

Day 1

Now that I'm here, I'm sure I will be all right. Everyone's really friendly and no one looks like the real outdoors type. I'm sharing a room with a girl called Claire.

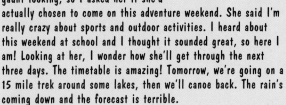

We talked a while before this evening's meal. She is thin, pale and gaunt looking, so I asked her if she'd actually chosen to come on this adventure weekend. She said I'm really crazy about sports and outdoor activities. I heard about this weekend at school and I thought it sounded great, so here I am! Looking at her, I wonder how she'll get through the next three days. The timetable is amazing! Tomorrow, we're going on a 15 mile trek around some lakes, then we'll canoe back. The rain's coming down and the forecast is terrible.

Day 2

The day was so full, Claire and I still didn't get a chance to talk much. When we were leaving this morning, Alice, our instructor, asked her why is your backpack twice the size of everyone else's? My strange roommate answered because I want to get really fit! Alice said leave a few things behind. Claire just shook her head and laughed.

I'm too tired to stay up writing about it all. Tomorrow we're going to do some climbing and abseiling. Aaagh!

Day 3

Well, the weekend is nearly over. Tonight, we're going to have a barbecue by the lake. Today was awesome. The abseiling was just as scary as I'd thought, and when it was all over, Alice told me you'll have to come back with Claire in the summer. You make a great team! When I asked her why, she said you're overcautious but Claire encourages you. Claire's reckless but you keep her in check.

At the barbecue, I got a chance to talk to Claire a bit more. She's amazing. I love doing all this she told me while we were stuffing our faces because I broke an arm and a leg in a skiing accident last winter and I got so fed up having to stay indoors all the time.

Home again

How was your weekend? everyone keeps asking me. I just say I was best at everything. You know me! What I don't tell them about is the nightmares I keep having.

A few hours after I'd gotten home, Claire called to ask if I want to go back to Great Rocks with her in August. Well I answered I'll think about it and phone you back soon. Oops, I don't have her phone number!

I stepped across the fast-running stream (as the picture shows).

There is no room left — I said: no room!

parentheses   hyphen   dash

Parentheses

Parentheses are pairs of curved lines which you use around words in order to separate them from the rest of a sentence.
For example:
My ant project is finished, but Jan's Dad (an insect specialist, as I found out) said he would look at it before I hand it in*.

Usually, the words in parentheses give extra detail or an explanation.

With parentheses, the punctuation depends on whether you choose to write the words in parentheses as part of a sentence or as a separate sentence.

If they are part of a sentence, any punctuation that belongs to the sentence goes outside the parentheses. For example:
Entries must reach us by May 22nd (any received later will not be valid).

If they form a separate sentence, the punctuation goes inside the parentheses:
Entries must reach us by May 22nd. (Entries received later will not be valid.)

Dashes

A dash is a short horizontal line used on its own or in pairs**. It is best avoided, especially in formal writing.

Dashes have about the same use as parentheses. In informal writing or in direct speech, you can use them instead of parentheses. Use two dashes if the extra words are in the middle of the sentence, as in *They want to visit Paris — I can see why — on their way to Geneva.* Use one dash if the extra words are at the end: *They want to visit Paris — I can understand why.*

Hyphens

A hyphen is like a dash, but shorter. Its main use is to join two or more words to show they should be read as one word with its own meaning. For example: *on-the-spot fines, short-term deal.*

Sometimes a hyphen is needed for compound words (a word made from two or more words), for example, *baby-sitter*. Others become accepted as new words that you write without a hyphen, such as *offsides, seaweed,* and *flashback.*

There are no firm rules to tell you when to join words up or when to link them with hyphens. You will often have to check compound words in a dictionary.

Hyphen guidelines

1 Use hyphens if the meaning is unclear or wrong without them:
A   *two-month-old kittens*
B   *two month-old kittens*

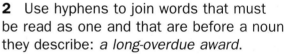

2 Use hyphens to join words that must be read as one and that are before a noun they describe: *a long-overdue award.*
3 Use a hyphen to join a verb ending in *ing* or *ed* with another word that changes its meaning. For example: *well-tuned, mind-boggling.* (The exception is if the other word ends in *ly*, when no hyphen is needed: *nicely worded.*)
4 Use a hyphen to join words with the same last and first letters: *grass-seed.*

In American English, more compound words are written as one word than in British English. For example: *night-time* (UK) but *nighttime* (US). As this shows, in American English, point 4 above is not always true.

Other uses

The hyphen is used to mean *to* in expressions like *1964-1982.*

Hyphens also go on the end of a line to break up a long word for which there is not enough room. Avoid this in your writing if you can. If you do it, break the word in a place which will not make reading difficult.

It is a pa-ragraph.

It is a para-graph.

*You can often use commas instead of parentheses. Use parentheses if they make the writing much clearer, as in this example.
**Never use other punctuation next to a dash.

Pirates aboard game

The story below has 19 numbered gaps. Use the board on the right to complete it. For each gap, look at the strip with the matching number and select the correct piece to fill the gap. (You will probably have to look some words up in a dictionary.)

Pirate MacClaw crept up the 1 to the galleon's deck. 2 Tom Puffin, who had rowed old MacClaw across from the 3 pirate ship 4 sick with fear all the way), shivered in the boat beneath.

5 MacClaw (who had celebrated his 6 the previous night) ran across the deserted deck toward the captain's quarters. He did not blink an 7 as he caught sight of the huge cages in which the galleon's captain was reputed to keep 8 and a 9 tiger. He had other things on his mind.

Soon he was creeping into Captain Cachou's cabin 10 was fast asleep on a 11 stool opposite the door. Unfortunately, MacClaw's parrot (who had been 12 on the old pirate's left shoulder ever since he had climbed on board the galleon) suddenly screeched, "Pirate MacClaw here!" This 13 went unheard, though, for the captain was in his 14 and his head was 15.

In the 16, the pirate had the 17 leather folder firmly in his large hands and was running back down toward Tom. The boy quietly sighed with relief (and wondered how he would ever have his 18 Mission accomplished, Tom rowed them into the peaceful, safe darkness, in which the blurred outlines of the 19 soon appeared.

Face painting

Where should you add one pair of parentheses in each of these seven instructions?

1. You will need face paints, two or three brushes and at least one sponge see Getting started on p.1.

2. Use water-based paints they cost more but give better results.

3. Sponge a yellow base onto the face brownish yellow if possible.

4. Sponge a white muzzle and chin lions have a white beard.

5. Paint a black nose joined to a black upper lip; also paint black lines around the eyes. See the illustration.

6. Paint bottom lip red and add black whiskers dots and lines as shown.

7. Brush hair up and back into a mane and sponge white streaks onto it. These will easily wash out.

MacCLAW'S MISSION

1	loosely tied rope ladder	loosely-tied rope ladder	loosely tied ropeladder
2	Mean while	Mean-while	Meanwhile,
3	nowinvisible	now invisible	now-invisible
4	(and who had felt	and who had felt	and (who had felt
5	Quietfooted	Quiet-footed	Quiet footed
6	seventieth birthday	seventieth birth day	seventieth birth-day
7	eye lid	eye-lid	eyelid
8	blood-hounds	bloodhounds	blood hounds
9	maneating	man eating	man-eating
10	— the guard	(the guard	— the guard —
11	three legged	threelegged	three-legged
12	solidly-perched	solidly perched	solidlyperched
13	ill timed squawk	illtimed squawk	ill-timed squawk
14	bathtub	bath-tub	bath tub
15	under water	under-water	underwater
16	twinkling of an eye	twinkling-of-an-eye	twinkling of an eye —
17	longdesired	long-desired	long desired
18	grand-pa's courage).	grandpa's courage.)	grandpa's courage).
19	pirate ship	pirate-ship	pirateship

55

If the layout of your writing (the way it is placed on the page) is cramped, it is hard to read. Here are some guidelines to help you present it neatly. You can also find out how to lay out letters.

Margins

Margins are the spaces which you leave on the left and right with no writing in them.

The left-hand margin should be straight (you can draw a line in with a ruler), and it is often a little wider than the right-hand margin. You can make the right-hand margin straight too, although you may end up with awkward gaps between the words.

Each new paragraph starts at the same distance from the left-hand margin.

Someone had to go down. The divers all looked terrified. Titch volunteered.

She lowered herself into the sea and let go of the ladder. She soon located the wreck, a gloomy shape beneath her. She found the right porthole. It was shut tight.

She tugged on the frame. All of a sudden, it was pushed from inside. An unknown diver's face appeared.

Paragraphs

A paragraph is a short section of writing within a longer piece. Each new paragraph starts a little way from the left margin (called indenting).

There are no rules to say where you should start a new paragraph. Usually, you do so when you move to a new subject or a new aspect of the same subject.

Formal letters

There are two styles to choose from.

Style 1: indented paragraphs
Address of person you are writing to

Your address

Fun Products
4 Creek Road
San Francisco, CA 94112

July 10, 1997 — **Date**

Robert Jensen
The Magic Shop
36 Park Avenue
Fort Worth, TX 76102-3722

Dear Mr. Jensen:

Colon
(***Dear Sir*** or ***Dear Madam*** **if you don't know the name)***

On June 6, I sent you a false mustache.

Please either let me know your response or return the sample to me.

Yours sincerely,
Katie Katz
Katie Katz

Sign, and type or write your name clearly.

Style 2: everything lined up on the left. This has become the most common form.

Fun Products
4 Creek Road
San Francisco, CA 94112

July 10, 1997

Robert Jensen
The Magic Shop
36 Park Avenue
Fort Worth, TX 76102-3722

Dear Mr. Jensen:

On June 6, I sent you a false mustache.

Leave some space between paragraphs.

Please either let me know your response or return the sample to me.

Yours sincerely,

Katie Katz
Katie Katz

Informal letters

For letters to friends or family, you can follow either style. You leave out the person's address, though, and you could also leave out your own. End with something like *With love from*, *See you soon* or *With best wishes*:

7 Mermaid Lane,
New York,
NY 11010-4123
August 12, 1995

Dear Ben,
The week in the country was wonderful. Many thanks once again for organizing it.
Did you find Lucy's leash? I'm sure I left it in your car. Please bring it down on Sunday.

Love to you all,
Ray

Envelopes

There are two possible styles for the address on an envelope:

Mrs. Wright
7 Briar Road
London NW6 4RD
Great Britain

Mr. Jensen
The Magic Shop
36 Park Avenue
Fort Worth, TX 76102-3722

Addresses

In letters and on envelopes, you write addresses without putting any punctuation on the ends of lines.

*If you don't know whether you are writing to a man or woman, put *Dear Sir/Madam*. In this case, end with *Yours faithfully*.
**Notice that this breaks the usual rule about starting new paragraphs away from the left margin.

Letter box

Lay out these two letters properly. Do letter 1 following style 1 and letter 2 following style 2 (see opposite page).

Letter 1

Date: May 7, 1997
From: you (at your own address)
To: the manager of an ice rink. You know the manager is a man, but you don't know his name.
The ice rink's address: Ice World, Cold Harbor Street, Tacoma, WA 98404-2371. What your letter says (write it in a single paragraph): I came skating yesterday and I forgot my shoes in the changing room. Please keep them for me if you find them. I will pick them up next week.

Letter 2

Date: May 6, 1997
From: you (at your own address)
To: Mrs. Graham, the manageress of a supermarket.
The supermarket's address: Cheapstore, 106 Kiln Road, Atlanta, GA 30307-1398. What your letter says (break this into two paragraphs): Last week, I bought a jar of instant coffee from Cheapstore which I had to return. The coffee had a thick layer of green mold on the top. Please, could you contact me about this matter as soon as possible? You said that I would hear from you within 48 hours, but I still have not.

Tiebreaker

To win trips to a city of their choice, the entrants in this competition had to give their reasons for wanting to go there. Here are the three winning entries. Can you split each one into three paragraphs?

Tiebreaker Competition

The city I most want to visit is Cairo. This is because the Sphinx and the Pyramids are just on the outskirts, and I would like to see them. I did a project on ancient Egypt and I built a model of the Sphinx. My model is small and new. I would like to stand in front of the real Sphinx, which is huge and ancient. Another reason for going to Cairo is to see the Nile. This is the longest river in the world, and if I visited Cairo, I could walk across it, using a bridge of course!

I am fascinated by buildings and one day I want to become an architect. I live on a cattle ranch in Oregon and I have never seen any tall buildings. The city I most want to visit is New York. Here I would see some of the oldest and most famous skyscrapers in the world. I could also see the wonderful skyline that they make. I have been saving my pocket money to go to New York for three years, but I still don't have enough. I hope I win this competition, because then I can go right away, and I can buy a camera with the money I have saved.

My best friend has moved to London, and my biggest hobby is history. Because of this, I want to visit London. My friend lives near the British Museum. He says it is full of exciting things to see, and wants to show me some seventh century Anglo-Saxon treasure there. I only know London from books. I would especially love to visit the Tower and the Houses of Parliament.

57

capital letters
(in red)

small or "lower
case" letters
(in blue)

Capitals checklist

Use a capital letter
• after a period, an exclamation point or a question mark*;
• to write the word *I* (meaning *me*);

Also use a capital letter at the start of
• a sentence;
• months, days of the week and special days: *in January, on Monday, Easter, Thanksgiving*;
• people's names and titles: *Jill Page, Mr. Fisher, Doctor Fellows, Queen Anne*. If *doctor* (or a title such as *queen, prince, duke* and so on) is used without a name, only use a capital letter if you are referring to the title of a particular person.

For example: *the Queen of England*. Use a lower case (small letter) when you are using a title in a general sense, such as: *every queen of England since 1700*;
• place names: *Sydney, California, Germany*. Words that are part of a place name start with a capital letter: *Great Salt Lake*. Words that come from place names: *a Californian, in German*;
• street names and names of buildings: *Park Lane, Ferry Street, the Eiffel Tower*;
• brand names and names of companies and organizations: *a Ford, Bird's Eye, the Foreign Office*;
• titles of books, films, songs and so on. You often also use a capital letter at the beginning of each important word in these titles: *The War of the Planets*.

Unwanted capitals

Do not use a capital letter
• at the start of the points of the compass (*Head north*!), unless they are part of a place name (*the North Pole*) or refer to a place (*the East*);
• for the seasons: *summer*.

Capital spy

Bill Spanner is jotting down a conversation that he is listening in to. Can you add the 36 capital letters that are needed?

i've arranged a meeting with two members of the dark shadow gang. it will be in a bar called the stag. it's on wincott street, just west of the junction with gilbert road, close to waterloo station. they've promised to come on monday at seven, on condition that i bring only you, prince baklava. we must not let anyone else know about this meeting, prince, and i mean that! don't tell princess baklava about it. they're a dangerous mob. they want us both there because they're hungarian and their english is not perfect. i can translate for you if necessary. be on time, please? we can meet in the street outside the stag. park your jaguar nearby and i'll look out for it. i'll wear my winter coat with the secret pockets, in case anything goes wrong.

Extras

Here are a few other signs and marks which you will see used.
[ ] Square brackets: these usually go around a comment that has been added to a piece of writing, as in They [the people she met in Mexico] are coming over.
& This sign is called an **ampersand**. It stands for and.
{ Brace: this can also be used the other way round:}. It is used in tables or notes to show the various parts of something. For example:

Subjects ⎰ Art
⎱ French
Physics

*If the period is used to show an abbreviation, there is no capital letter after it: *See you Tues. morning.*
Exclamation points and question marks can be followed by a small letter in direct speech (see page 52).

Page 35

Testing correspondence

There are nine periods, ten commas, one colon, one semicolon, one exclamation point, two hyphens, one question mark, one apostrophe and four quotation marks.

Pages 36-37

Pen problems

*I'll be home late from school today, **Mom**. After volleyball practice, Miss Mussly wants to discuss plans for our sports **day**. See you at about six **p.m**.*
*(Please feed Misty as soon as you get **in**. Because of the kittens, I don't think she should have to wait until **six**.)*

Costly dots

SORRY I LET YOU DOWN IN **INVERNESS**. I'LL EXPLAIN WHEN I SEE **YOU**. MY WALLET WAS STILL IN YOUR BACKPACK WHEN YOU LEFT IN A **HUFF**. PLEASE MEET ME FORT WILLIAM STATION ON SAT 8PM RIGHT OF LUGGAGE LOCKERS.

Drifter's diary

*Up at 11 **a.m**. I didn't **take a bath**. **My** sisters had left the bathroom in such a state that I didn't feel like **it**. I went over to Jo Drone's Café for a hotdog because Dad was retiling the kitchen **floor**. I just love that hot-yellow **mustard**. Teeny Tina came by for me later and we spent the whole afternoon at the **D.J. Club**. On my way home I bumped into my old classmate Sally Straite in Suburb **Lane**. **When** I told her about how bored I felt, she told me to pull myself together and perhaps get a summer **job**. **She** suggested I start by keeping a **diary**. Sally thinks that problems I have to iron out will soon become **clear**. All I have to do is keep a diary for a few days and then read it **through**. **She** reckons the problems will soon leap off the page at **me**.*
*Sally's **tel**. number is 666 3333. **She** said I can call her whenever I need some moral **support**. I'm going to clean up the bathroom **now**. **Then** I'm going to take a bath and go to **bed**. It's 10:00 **p.m**.*

Pointless

The four sentences which should end with a full stop are 2, 3, 4 and 9.

Dotty dramas

*I read the article in yesterday's Echo about the great pearl **robbery**. I was on that train and am writing to let you know what I **know**. **There** were hardly any passengers on the **train**. **In** my carriage, there was only one **man**. I noticed him because he had six briefcases and looked very **nervous**. I soon dozed **off**. **All** of a sudden, I woke up to the sound of terrible **shouts**. A woman with a black mask over her face rushed toward me and threw a pile of shrimp and mayonnaise sandwiches in my face and all over my **clothes**. **Then** she climbed out of the window onto the **platform**. **The** woman disappeared into the night while I started trying to clean off the shrimp and mayonnaise. **At** this point, I discovered there were lots of blue pearls mixed in with the **food**. I scraped as much as I could into a plastic bag and got off the **train**. **Nobody** noticed me go in all the **commotion**. **Now** that I have read about what happened to the man with the briefcases, I want to hand in the **pearls**. **You** can phone me on 867 2382.*

Page 39

Two by two

A The apples, which were red, had worms in them.
B The apples which were red had worms in them.
C The boys who were wearing red all had black hair.
D The boys, who were wearing red, all had black hair.
E The ham, which was cold, came with salad.
F The ham which was cold came with salad.

A comma or two

1 My brother is **lazy**, rude and arrogant.
2 Many people will read this **story**, although it is very badly written.
3 Stefie has brought **flowers**, ice cream and chocolates.
4 **Meanwhile**, Susie was cycling home.
5 I took the books which were **old**, torn and **shabby**, but left the good ones for my mother.
6 The three bands that were playing were Sound and **Emotion**, Billy and the **Cheesemakers**, and the Blue Moon Band.
7 He waved at **Lisa**, who was watching from the **window**, and walked down the street.
8 The soccer **players**, who were **exhausted**, limped off the field together.

Lily's list

*Pharmacy: new **toothbrush**, aspirin and soap.*
*Butcher's: **sausages**, bacon and a leg of lamb.*
*Supermarket: **milk, butter, eggs, flour, sugar, pasta**, cans of sardines, and ice cream.*
*Greengrocer's: **apples, pears, bananas, beans**, carrots and broccoli.*
Baker's: five dinner rolls and two loaves of bread.
*Hardware store: six **short**, sturdy nails and a small hammer.*

Page 39 continued

Comma commotion

These Cosifit earmuffs are warm, **comfortable and** suitable for anyone from 6 to 60! The adjustable head strap means that **however big** or small your head may be, Cosifit ear**muffs will** always fit!

This latest addition to the **Supertec computer game** series is the most exciting, challenging and **absorbing yet!** Can you help Hoghero in his desperate **battle for** control of the universe? Help him stop **Miteymouse from** conquering the world!

Every **trendy teenager** needs a Staralarm! When you go to bed, just set the alarm by choosing a time and a voice - the voice of your **favorite pop** star. What better way to wake up than to the sound of Kool Malone, **Freddy** and the Freezers or Ritchy Roon?

Pages 40-41

Mix and match

Andy and his parents have moved to Gap,/ which is in France.

Jan and her family have moved to Arcola/, which is in Canada.

I thought it over/ and quickly decided on a course of action.

He gave me some sound advice,/ but I still could not make up my mind.

In the late afternoon,/ I decided to go to the police station.

After the detective's visit/, I no longer felt in the mood to work.

The man wrinkled up his nose in disdain/, then grudgingly guided them down the dark alley.

The woman looked down her nose at them,/ but agreed to show them the documents.

Stop gap

1 Live coverage of this fascinating sporting event will begin on Radio Livewire **at 6:00**.
2 There were **18,000** people at the **concert**, so our chances of bumping into **Gemma**, Jim and Sam were very **slight**.
3 **Disheartened**, the explorers began their return **journey**, setting **off**...
4 In early Roman **times**, theaters were built of **wood**.
5 At **last, wet**, gasping and **exhausted**, they reached the bus **shelter**.
6 The **sun**, which we had not seen for two **months**, blinded **us**.

Printer problems

Nearly all wild cats live in **rainforests**. They hunt and eat **meat**. They have very good **eyesight**, and often...

(**Cathy**, *please research all the general points for the above opening* **paragraph**. *When you have done* **so, write** *them up on my* **computer**. *The file name is* **WCL**.)

The tiger is the largest **cat**. It is extremely **strong**. It hunts for its **food**, catching large animals if it **can**. Rather than go **hungry, though**, it eats small creatures such as **frogs, ants, worms,** beetles and so on.

(**Cathy**, *please also research and write the section on* **leopards**. *I have gathered the relevant* **books, folders, cuttings,** *etc. You will find them all on my* **desk,** *to the left of the pile of parrot* **leaflets**.)

Hasty homework

For my summer **vacation**, I went to **Agadir**, a beach paradise in Morocco. I stayed in a luxury hotel with three enormous swimming **pools**, a **movie theater**, dance clubs, a jogging track and a computer games room.

The hotel is by a **beautiful, long,** white beach (OR beautiful long white beach), and the bedrooms which have balconies overlook the sea. My Mom and Dad had a hard time getting to sleep because of the waves crashing down below. My **room**, which had no balcony and was just around the **corner**, was quiet.

I did not like the pools as much as the **sea**, although they did have lots of truly awesome water **rapids**, waves and whirlpools. The two swimming pools which have lots of sun loungers around them are always crowded. Because the third one has lanes in it for serious **swimming**, it is usually empty. On the **beach**, there were huge waves, which I loved. One morning after a **storm**, I saw some jellyfish on the beach.

The food was wonderful. The hotel has chefs from all over the **world**, so we mostly ate Chinese food and Moroccan **food**, which were our favorites.

Even though we only spent a day **there**, our visit to Marrakesh was the highlight of the whole vacation. It is a really exciting **town**, and the markets and tiny ancient streets (OR **tiny**, ancient streets) are full of weird things like **carpets**, olives and spices all piled **up**, leather bags and sandals.

Because it was spring and the weather was not too **hot**, I really enjoyed this vacation.

Page 43

Fishy prizes

For the pastry, you will **need:** flour, butter [...]
For the filling, have ready the **following:** fresh shrimp, shelled; crab **meat,** either fresh or from a **can;** cream, eggs and seasoning. [...]

[...] The ingredients for the cheese sauce **are:** equal amounts of milk, cream and yogurt; a tablespoon of flour; finely grated cheddar cheese; two beaten egg yolks. Stir these [...] Don't include the **cheese:** this must go in after the sauce has thickened and is off the heat. To assemble the **pie,** do the following: put half the potato in the bottom of an ovenproof dish; place the fish mixture on top, making sure it is well spread over all the potato; cover with the remaining **potato;** finally, pour the cheese sauce [...]

For the fishcakes, mash together these **ingredients:** poached cod, boiled potatoes and two raw eggs. Add [...] Include parsley and chives, and one of the **following:** dill, fennel, sorrel. Also add a knob of butter. Shape this mixture into [...]

For the **sauce,** mince some peeled shrimp and mix with lots of sour cream.

[...] As a main course, serve with boiled new potatoes and **broccoli;** as a snack, serve with crusty bread.

Getting it right

*Washomatic for sale. This machine is a genuine bargain: it is only 12 years old; there is not a single visible patch of rust on **it**; last but not least, it does not leak. Phone Johnny on 324-5543.*

*Attention, old pen collectors: Green Silhouette pen for sale, 1952 model. Features **included**: original case, gold nib, embossed logo. Phone Pipa Pentop, 324-5682.*

*For sale or **rent**: garage in Bach Alley. Contact Mrs. Lucas, 3 Bach Square.*

Wanted: *young person to deliver newspapers in Combe Park area. Must have own bike. Apply to Nat's News. Gardener sought. The following qualifications are **required**: familiarity with Supermow, sound knowledge of organic vegetable growing and garden pest control. Phone 324-3344.*

Hair excesses

Come to **us** for a wide range of hair care: perms, hair straightening, coloring, highlighting, beading, hair extensions. Our perms are perfect in every way: gentle, **lasting** and adapted to suit your face shape. Choose between three wonderful shampoos: frosted yogurt and banana for dry hair; lemon and lime cocktail for greasy hair; finally, for problem hair, mango and chili revitalizing **magic** or Brazil nut balsam. Always follow up a shampoo with a good conditioner: this guarantees good hair condition. Among our dozens of choices, we recommend **either** deep action strawberry, marigold petal extract or luxury oatmilk.

Treat yourself **to** a head massage, the ideal treatment for tired heads. You get a 15 minute massage given by an expert; generous amounts of the best head massage oils; a shampoo and blow dry.

We give you the hairdo you want. Once you have it, you will want to keep it; to help you, we stock 30 varieties of hair spray. Also in stock: hundreds of mousses, hair **gels** and styling spritzes.

Pages 44-45

Ask a straight question

Only number 1 is an indirect question: *I asked her if she could bring him to my party.* All the others need a question mark on the end.

Awkward questions

1 Do you live here?
2 Where were you at eleven o'clock last night?
3 What are the names of the four friends who were watching TV with you?
4 Did you or one of your friends hear anything unusual?
5 Do you have a friend called Jack?
6 Was he here last night?
7 Have you heard of the Burly Gang, a gang of thugs who hang around the neighborhood?
8 Hasn't Jack ever mentioned them to you or boasted about being their leader?
9 Why did you lie when I asked you if you had heard anything unusual?
10 Was it you who gave Jack the key to your parents' garage so he could hide there last night?

Searching questions

*One day, you'll leave, won't **you**?*
When I asked you last summer,
You said you'd be true,
*But now, I just **wonder**.*
Why is it always me
*That gets left **behind**?*
In this state, I can't see
*How life can ever be **kind**?*

*Friends are no **better**.*
Why are they never around
*When I need a **shoulder**?*
*Oh, when will I stop feeling so **blue**?*

Questionnaire mix-up

2b), 3a), 4c), 5a), 6a), 7b), 8c), 9a), 10b).

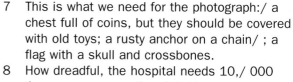

Pages 46-47

Overkill

1

What a **calamity!** Dire is to lose its railway station bathroom unless urgent action is taken. This, at least, is what the Association of Dire Residents (ADR) fear, following their meeting with the Station's Passenger Liaison Committee (SPLC) yesterday.

According to the ADR spokesperson, Gail Bigwail, the Committee is intent on cutting costs. Losing the bathroom will save exactly the amount they are looking for.

What an unnecessary, backward **step!** The shortest journey from Dire is 23 minutes, and with no bathroom at Dire Central, passengers would just have to keep their legs **crossed!**

We agree with Ivor Right, also of the ADR, who points out that, with a little thought and care, small savings could be made here and there, thus allowing the bathroom to be kept open. How true, Mr. Right, and how eagerly we will publicize your views! The ADR is planning a Day of Action in the near future. So cheer up, Citizens of **Dire, buy** the Dire Echo every **day, and** we will keep you **informed!**

Surprise, surprise

1 Wow, you DO have a brain after **all!** I suppose I'm **impressed,** though it's pretty horrible having to admit **it.** See you on Saturday, Einstein. Charlie

2 Great stuff, Miss **Brainypants!** After Lady Banstead's stunning **announcement,** I can only beg to remain your proud best **friend.** See you at volleyball, clever socks! Di

3 **Congratulations, Dawn!** The whole school is proud of **you.** Best wishes for next year, Helga Banstead

4 Dear Dawn, You brilliant **girl!** I just can't get over how clever you **are,** and I'm dying to get home from this wretched business trip so I can give you the hug you **deserve.**

Watch your brothers. Charlie will be green with envy but OK. Jamie will hate you getting all the attention! See you on Saturday. Lots of love, Mom

Slot machine roundup

1 Toward the end of the meal/, the waiter got so slow that we had to leave/ without having a dessert.

2 Toward the end of the meal,/the café really did get very full,/ didn't it?

3 We asked them if/ they had decided to go home or/ if they had gone to the club.

4 I wonder/ if he thinks /their boat will dock in Singapore.

5 When/ does he think/ their boat will dock in Singapore?

6 To put on the show, we asked for four props/ : a pair of stilts, a clown's outfit, an overcoat/ and a bucket.

7 This is what we need for the photograph:/ a chest full of coins, but they should be covered with old toys; a rusty anchor on a chain/ ; a flag with a skull and crossbones.

8 How dreadful, the hospital needs 10,/ 000 times more money than/ that!

9 The current rate for grape picking is 10/ times more than/ he paid us last summer.

Pages 48-49

Filling the gap

1 His **parents'** house is in Armadillo.

2 Their **children's** bedrooms are all in the attic.

3 We ended up in the **town's** worst diner.

4 My **team's** colors are scarlet, blue and yellow.

5 My favorite **band's** annual tour starts next week.

6 Mrs. **Jones's** next-door neighbor is a retired filmstar.

7 Of this **ship's** two radios, only one is working.

8 The conductor would not let us onto the **bus's** top deck.

9 By the end of the match, the 13 **players'** energy had completely run out.

10 The **Browns'** garage had been emptied overnight.

Get the facts right

2 the woman's umbrellas

3 the hamster's carrots

4 the cooks' spoons

5 the policemen's motorcycle

6 the girl's sandwiches

7 the friends' surfboard

8 the mice's hole

9 the butcher's knives

10 the dogs' bone

11 the thieves' bags

12 the boys' CD player

Photo album

The sentences which match the pictures are:
A1, B1, C2, D2, E1 and F2.

Pages 50-51

Itsy-bitsy

Like all spiders, **it** has eight legs. **Its** overall length is about that of a human hand. The web **it** makes out of **its** own silk is so strong that even small animals get trapped in **it**. **It's** not able to eat solid food, so **it** fills **its** prey with special juices to turn **it** into liquid **it** can eat.

Chatterbox contractions

Maria's paintbrushes **are not** in the same box as yours.

The baker's is closed and the supermarket **does not** sell Mr. Duff's doughnuts.

It is not worth mending my tennis racket: all its strings are broken and the **handle is** cracked.

I **will not** be allowed to come unless **you will** give me a lift home.

There is nothing on that **they would** really like to see.

Its streets are so quiet and dull, especially when **it is** raining.

I would rather go to Suzie's, if **she is** home.

They had all gone by the time we got there.

That **baker is** a surly man.

They have gone to the doctor's.

Filling apostrophes

Is going to the **dentist's** a nightmare for your child? Come to us. **We're** the **children's** specialists. Some dentists terrify kiddies. **It's** their approach **that's** all wrong. Ours is sensitive and fun. Our offices look like **kids'** playrooms, but **they're** equipped with the latest technology so **everything's** as quick, painless and easy as possible - even fillings are fun here. **There's** constant music and we tell the kids spooky or fun stories while we work. **We'll** take good care of your **children's** health and looks without causing fear and tears!

Crime busters

1	**Harris**	7	**parents'**	13	**key's**
2	**Harrises'**	8	**dogs'**	14	**parents'**
3	**key**	9	**It's**	15	**its**
4	**bungalow's**	10	**They're**	16	**it's**
5	**door's**	11	**they**	17	**parents**
6	**doors**	12	**dogs**	18	**doors**
				19	**bungalows**

Page 53

What was that?

She said, "Right, put your pens down now, please!"
He said, "Carol's taken my pen."
She said, "I've left my lunch box at home!"
He said, "Jamie was copying Tracy's answers."
She said, "I can't believe how hard that was!"
She asked, "Did you hear about Ros and Kate?"

"Right, put your pens down now, please!" she said.
"Carol's taken my pen," he said.
"I've left my lunch box at home!" she said.
"Jamie was copying Tracy's answers," he said.

"I can't believe how hard that was!" she said.
"Did you hear about Ros and Kate?" she asked.

Adventure diary

This is where the quotation marks should go:

Day 1 [...] She **said**, "I'm really crazy about sports and outdoor activities. I heard about this weekend through school and I thought it sounded great, so here I **am**!" Looking at her [...]

Day 2 [...] Alice, our instructor, asked **her**, "Why is your backpack twice the size of everyone **else's**?" My strange roommate **answered**, "Because I want to get really **fit**!"
Alice **said**, "Leave a few things **behind**." Claire just [...]

Day 3 [...] Alice told **me**, "You'll have to come back with Claire in the summer. You make a great **team**!" When I asked her why, she **said**, "You're overcautious but Claire encourages you. Claire's reckless but you keep her in **check**."
[...] She's amazing. "I love doing all **this**," she told me while we were stuffing our **faces**, "because I broke an arm and a leg in a skiing accident last winter and I got so fed up having to stay indoors all the **time**."
[...] "How was your **weekend**?" everyone keeps asking me. I just **say**, "I was best at everything. You know **me**!" What I don't tell them about [...]
[...] with her in August. "Well," I **answered**, "I'll think about it and phone you back **soon**."
Oops, I don't have her phone number!

Page 55

Pirates aboard game

1 loosely-tied rope ladder
2 Meanwhile,
3 now-invisible
4 (and who had felt
5 Quiet-footed
6 seventieth birthday
7 eyelid
8 bloodhounds
9 man-eating
10 — the guard
11 three-legged
12 solidly perched
13 ill-timed squawk
14 bathtub
15 underwater
16 twinkling of an eye
17 long-desired
18 grandpa's courage).
19 pirate ship

Page 55 continued

Face painting

1   You will need face paints, two or three brushes and at least one sponge (**see** Getting started on **p.1**).
2   Use water-based paints (**they** cost more but give better **results).**
3   Sponge a yellow base onto the face (**brownish** yellow if **possible).**
4   Sponge a white muzzle and chin (**lions** have a white **beard).**
5   Paint a black nose joined to a black upper lip; also paint black lines around the eyes. (**See** the **illustration.)**
6   Paint bottom lip red and add black whiskers (**dots** and lines as **shown).**
7   Brush hair up and back into a mane and sponge white streaks onto it. (**These** will easily wash **out.)**

Page 57

Letter box

Your address

May 7, 1997

Ice World
Cold Harbor Street
Tacoma, WA 98404-2311

Dear Sir:

I came skating yesterday and I left my shoes in the changing room. Please keep them for me if you find them. I will pick them up next week.

Yours faithfully,
your signature
your name, clearly written

---

your address
May 6, 1997

Mrs Graham
Cheapstore
106 Kiln Road
Atlanta, GA 30307-1398

Dear Mrs Graham,

Last week, I bought a jar of instant coffee from Cheapstore which I had to return. The coffee had a thick layer of green mold on the top.

Please could you contact me about this matter as soon as possible? You said that I would hear from you within 48 hours, but I still have not.

Yours sincerely,

your signature
your name, clearly written

Tiebreaker

The city I most w<u>a</u>nt to visit is Cairo. This is because the Sphinx and the Pyramids are just on the outskirts, and I would like to see them.

I did a project on ancient Egypt and I built a model of the Sphinx. My model is small and new. I would like to stand in front of the real Sphinx, which is huge and ancient.

Another reason for going to Cairo is to see the Nile. This is the longest river in the world, and if I visited Cairo, I could walk across it, using a bridge of course!

I am fascinated by buildings and one day I want to become an architect. I live on a cattle ranch in Oregon and I have never seen any tall buildings.

The city I most want to visit is New York. Here I would see some of the oldest and most famous skyscrapers in the world. I could also see the wonderful skyline that they make.

I have been saving my pocket money to go to New York for three years, but I still have not got enough. I hope I win this competition, because then I can go right away and I can buy a camera with the money I have saved.

My best friend has moved to London, and my biggest hobby is history. Because of this, I want to visit London.

My friend lives near the British Museum. He says it is full of exciting things to see and wants to show me some seventh century Anglo-Saxon treasure there.

I only know London from books. I would especially love to visit the Tower and the Houses of Parliament.

Page 58

Capital spy

I've arranged a meeting with two members of the **Dark Shadow Gang**. It will be in a bar called the **Stag**. It's on **Wincott Street**, just west of the junction with **Gilbert Road**, close to **Waterloo Station**. They've promised to come on **Monday** at seven, on condition that I bring only you, **Prince Baklava**. We must not let anyone else know about this meeting, **Prince**, and I mean that! **Don't** tell **Princess Baklava** about it. They're a dangerous mob. They want us both there because they're **Hungarian** and their **English** is not perfect. I can translate for you if necessary. Be on time, won't you? We can meet in the street outside the **Stag**. Park your **Jaguar** nearby and I'll look for it. I'll wear my winter coat with the secret pockets, in case anything goes wrong.

GRAMMAR

CONTENTS

Them books or *those books*? *You was* or you *were*? It is often difficult to know how to put your words together correctly, but this book will help you improve your grammar skills. It contains fun puzzles that give you lots of practice, as well as simple explanations and guidelines to help you with tricky grammar points.

What is grammar?

Grammar is the way you use words and put them together into sentences that everyone can understand. The rules of grammar help you build sentences that make sense to other people. They tell you how to put words in the right order and use them correctly.

To use these rules correctly, you need to know about the different types of words that make up our language.

Why is grammar important?

To make yourself completely understood, you need to know the rules about things like word order. Putting things in the wrong place can completely change the meaning of a sentence:

Ann ate the fish. **The fish ate Ann.**

This book will help you avoid mistakes that could make people misunderstand what you are trying to say.

It will also help you improve your English. In everyday situations (when talking or writing to family or friends), people often say things that are not strictly correct. In formal situations, though, like interviews or exams, it is important to use your language correctly.

Besides, even little mistakes like getting one word wrong can change your meaning:

The owner of the car, which was enormous, polished it proudly.

The owner of the car, who was enormous, polished it proudly.

Using this book

On pages 67-71 you can find out about the different types of words that make up our language. Knowing about these will help you understand grammar and use it correctly.

On pages 72-90 there are simple explanations and guidelines to help you with tricky points that people often get wrong. For each double page, read the guidelines first, then test yourself with the puzzles. Try all of these, even ones that look easy. They may make something show up that you have not understood. This is not a write-in book, so you will need paper and a pen or pencil to write your answers down. You can check your answers on pages 91-95.

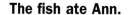

Watch out for boxes like this one. They contain guidelines and tests on confusing pairs or groups of words that people often slip up on (such as *to* and *too*).

Changing grammar

English grammar is constantly changing. This is because new ways of saying things become accepted, and difficult points that people find hard to follow are forgotten. This book does not deal with difficult areas that few people know about. It concentrates instead on common problems and mistakes that actually make what you write or say seem wrong.

In Britain and America, grammar has developed in different ways, so there are many small differences in the way British and American people speak English. For example: a British person might say, "Have you got a pen?" but an American would say, "Do you have a pen?"

Similarly, people from different parts of one country often speak in slightly different ways, called **dialects***.*

dog funny Nouns and adjectives Jim lonely

Here, and on the next four pages, you can learn the names for different types of words and find out about the jobs they do in a sentence. You can test what you have learned by doing the puzzles.

Nouns
A **noun** is a word which names a thing, a place, a person or an animal:

drum

Egypt

A noun can be **singular** (when naming one thing, as in *cat*) or **plural** (when naming more than one, as in *cats*).

A noun often has a small introducing word called an **article** (*the*, *a* or *an*) in front. For example: <u>the</u> sea, <u>a</u> car. Nouns which are names of people (and many that are place names) do not have articles in front. For example: *Katie, France, New York.*

Adjectives
An **adjective** is a describing word. It tells you what a noun is like. For example, it can tell you what something looks like, or how big it is. Numbers can also be adjectives: they tell you how many things are being talked about. Here are some common adjectives: *red, large, excellent, ugly.*

Jumbled nouns

Can you complete this story by unscrambling the jumbled nouns?

(Use the picture clues below to help you.)

Four criminals were arrested yesterday in **Pisar** after they tried to steal the Mona Lisa. Pretending to be **ranclees**, the thieves persuaded museum officials to let them remove the priceless **gnapinit**. However, as they were leaving the building, a **clamponie** recognized them as known villains, and the crooks dropped their loot and ran for it. The museum's revolving **rodos** proved to be more than they had bargained for, though. The doors jammed halfway around, and when a passing police **nav** stopped to investigate, **sodg** were able to surround the trapped villains. They are now firmly locked up in **rosnip**, and the famous picture is back in place ready for the weekend **russitot**.

Pisar   ranclees   gnapinit

clamponie   rodos   nav

sodg   rosnip   russitot

Give and take

Find four nouns and three adjectives in sentences 1 to 4. Then write out sentences A to D, completing them with the nouns and adjectives you have found.

1 **Bangkok is often very busy.**
2 **Sarah ran away screaming.**
3 **A black dog was barking loudly.**
4 **The rusty bicycle finally collapsed.**

A **They had bought the ... old car in ... .**
B **Where is ... today?**
C **Outside the house stood a shiny ... .**
D **I'm too ... to take the ... for a walk today.**

67

Verbs

A **verb** is an action word. It tells you what someone or something is doing. For example: *She is working*. Verbs can also show a state (*We live here, He is ill*).

Verbs are very important. They can turn a meaningless group of words (*lions deer*) into an actual sentence*: *Lions attack deer*.

A verb can also tell you about a past action (*They attacked*) or a future action (*They will attack*). There are different forms, or **tenses**, for talking about past, present and future actions. Verbs also change depending on who or what is doing the action (*I attack, He attacks*).

Subject and Object

The person or thing that does an action is called the **subject**. For example, in the sentence *Tim left the house*, *Tim* is the subject. In *He lives next door*, *He* is the subject.

The person or thing that is affected by the action is called the **object**. There are two kinds of objects. A **direct object** is affected directly by an action (for example, *the letter* in the sentence *Matthew sent the letter*). An **indirect object** is usually the person or thing that receives the direct object (like *his sister* in *Matthew sent the letter to his sister*).

Pronouns

A **pronoun** is a word you use to replace a noun. Here are some common ones: *I, me, she, it, we, us, them, mine, his, yours*.

Pronouns make language less repetitive. For example, think of two sentences like these: *The frightened girl peered outside. She saw three*

men waiting below. Without the pronoun *she*, you would have to repeat *the frightened girl*, which would sound very clumsy.

To do the puzzles on these pages, you may need to look back at some of the things that are explained on page 67.

──── **Pronoun fillers** ────

Some pronouns are missing from the report below. Read it through and then decide which pronoun each number stands for.

A yellow lesser-spotted, flat-billed frogcatcher, previously thought to be extinct, has been spotted in the Ice-pie National Park on the east coast. ..1.. was identified by keen birdwatcher Caesar Lotterfeather. ..2.. said yesterday, "..3.. had been out watching with a couple of friends, and as ..4.. were setting off home, ..1.. walked out right in front of us." Caesar said ..2.. and his friends were amazed to see the bird so near ..5.. .

"..3..'ve been coming here for twenty years but until now ..3..'ve only ever seen seagulls and the odd tern. ..4.. couldn't believe our eyes when we saw the frogcatcher cleaning its feet right in front of ..6.. ." Caesar was looking forward to reporting back to his wife. "..7.. is always telling ..8.. that ..3.. am wasting my time watching birds. Now ..3.. can really prove to ..9.. that my hobby's worthwhile."

*For more about sentences, see page 72.

Identity parade

In the list below there are five verbs, five nouns, and five words that can be either. Decide which group each word belongs to. Then fit the words that can be either verbs or nouns into sentences 1 to 5.

scream	follow	window
undo	study	hope
add	desk	wander
write	fly	shirt
climb	drawer	girl

1 My sister is hoping to ... art at college.
2 We managed to ... up onto the ridge of the mountain.
3 Her only ... now is that the train is running late.
4 When the man jumped out from behind the door, she let out a loud ... .
5 Mark swatted the ... that kept buzzing around the room.

Sentence spinner

Each ring of this circle contains a jumbled sentence. Rearrange the words in the rings so that each word is in the section labeled with its grammar name. Now you can find five sentences by reading clockwise around the circle, starting with a pronoun each time.

Which sentence still makes sense when its object and subject are swapped over?

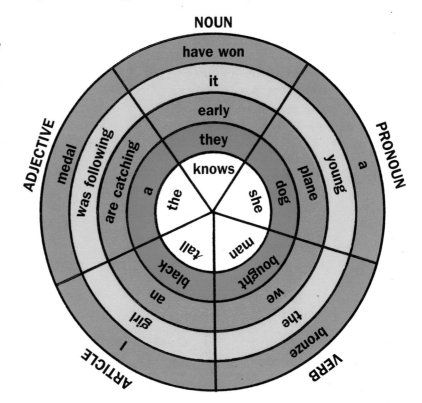

A sack of words

Arrange the words in this sack into five lists, putting all the nouns, verbs, adjectives, pronouns and articles together.

postcard
unhappy   sunny   will buy
to cry   she   is working
we   an   they
the   to dream
song   Louise
you
computer   waited   loud
beauty   a

🥜 affect/effect

What is the difference between the words *affect* and *effect*? One is a verb and one is usually a noun, but which is which? Check by looking in a dictionary, then decide which one should go in each of the sentences below.

1 What is the ... of adding flour to water?
2 That movie was really good. There were lots of special ...s.
3 I had a cold, but it didn't really ... me very badly.
4 Her illness had a very bad ... on her test results.
5 The weather can ... the way you feel.

69

Adverbs

An **adverb** is like an adjective, but instead of describing a noun or a pronoun, it tells you more about a verb, an adjective, or even another adverb. An adverb describes how, when or where something happens.

Here are some examples using adverbs: *He smiled <u>politely</u>, Liz drives <u>slowly</u>, We arrived <u>late</u>, Jo lives <u>there</u>, I'm <u>only</u> joking.*

Conjunctions

A **conjunction** is a linking word. It joins other words and groups of words together. Without conjunctions, sentences sound short and jerky. For example: *He closed his eyes. He didn't fall asleep.* The conjunction *but* can turn these into a single sentence: *He closed his eyes, <u>but</u> he didn't fall asleep.*

Here are some common conjunctions: *and, but, or, yet, therefore, so, because, although, while.*

Prepositions

A **preposition** is a word that tells you how one thing is related to another. It is normally attached to a noun or a pronoun.

A lot of prepositions show where one thing is in relation to another. For example: *The dog is lying <u>on</u> the bed.*

Other prepositions show when something happens in relation to something else. For example: *Mike's parents are coming to stay <u>before</u> Christmas.*

Here are some common prepositions: *in, on, under, to, before, after, around, near, down, over, up, past, between, into.*

Lots of verbs look as if they are followed by prepositions (for example, *to break <u>down</u>, to cheer <u>up</u>, to break <u>in</u>*), but in fact, in these cases, these little words are thought of as part of the verb.

Doubling up

Some words can do one job in one sentence, and a different one elsewhere. So, depending on the job they are doing, they can belong to different groups of words. Here are some examples:

1 *Her* and words like *this* and *that* can be pronouns (*Look at <u>her</u>; <u>That</u>'s a pity*) and also adjectives (*It is <u>her</u> jacket; Look at <u>that</u> coat*).

2 Some words, like *hard, late* and *fast*, can be adverbs (*They ran <u>fast</u>; The train arrived <u>late</u>*) or adjectives (*Andy is a <u>fast</u> runner; We are getting a <u>late</u> train*).

3 Words like *so* and *however* can be conjunctions (*He wasn't in, <u>so</u> I left; I am fine, <u>however</u> Jane is not very well*) or adverbs (*I am <u>so</u> tired; <u>However</u> hard he works, he won't pass his exams now*).

—— Scrambled ——

Unjumble the prepositions below, then decide which one fits each sentence:

1 **My car was parked ... the truck and the motorcycle.**
2 **They walked home ... the party.**
3 **The dog jumped ... the lake.**
4 **The prisoner ran as fast as he could ... the bridge.**
5 **The money was hidden ... the cupboard.**

70

Sentence building

Put these parts of sentences together into the most likely pairs, joining each pair with one of the conjunctions shown in blue.

He couldn't remember her name,

she was jogging.

He forced the door open

crept quietly into the house.

looked for the car,

it had already gone.

Michelle rushed to the window and

he had met her before.

my knee hurts.

I can't play tennis today

She listened to music on her headphones

while | because | but | and | although

borrow/lend teach/learn

People often confuse these words. Borrowing is when you take something from someone for a while, but lending is when you give something for a while.

Teaching means showing someone how to do something, or telling them about it. Learning means finding out.

Decide which verb (*borrow, lend, teach* or *learn*) fits each speech bubble.

Did you ... my shoes again last night?

He is going to ... to speak Spanish before he goes.

Do I have to ... him some money?

She is trying to ... me to sing.

Sentence parts

The sentences below have been split into parts. Write them out, circling each part in the right color to show which grammar group it belongs to.

noun (subject)	article
noun (object)	verb
pronoun(subject)	adverb
pronoun (object)	conjunction
adjective	preposition

1 The / dog / ran / into / the / road, / and / the / car / just / missed / it.
2 We / are having / a / big / party, / so / you / must come.
3 The / big / bear / escaped / from / the / zoo / and / was / never / seen / again.
4 The / dancers / were / so / shocked, / they / had to stop / the / show.

Fill the gap

Choose the correct adjectives or adverbs from the lists below to fill in the gaps in this story. (Use each once only.)

As Ian stepped into the house and wiped his ..1.. shoes on the mat, he heard a ..2.. crash from upstairs. He closed the door ..3.. and waited, trembling. There was no sound. Ian crept across the  **..4.. hallway, his heart pounding ..5.. . He tiptoed up the ..6.. stairs, moving ..7.. from one to the next. On the landing, he paused and held his breath. He could just hear a ..8.. sound coming from the sitting room. Ian breathed in ..9.., rested his trembling hand on the door and then ..10.. flung it open. As ..11.. faces appeared all around the room, the lights went on, and a chorus of familiar voices cried ..12.., "Happy Birthday!" Ian sank ..13.. into a chair.**

Adjectives: cheerful, loud, muddy, empty, creaky, faint

Adverbs: merrily, thankfully, quietly, deeply, heavily, lightly, suddenly

71

A sentence is a group of words that makes sense on its own. Most sentences have a subject and a verb. For example: *The cat ran across the garden*. Short exclamations, questions and greetings are also sentences, even though they have no subject or verb. For example: *How amazing! What? Good morning*. A sentence always starts with a capital letter and ends with a period (.), question mark (?) or exclamation point (!).

Clauses and phrases

Sentences can be made up of **clauses** (groups of words that contain verbs) and **phrases** (groups of words without verbs).

A phrase adds extra meaning to a sentence.	A main clause makes sense on its own.

In a panic, she ripped up the letter that he had written.

A subordinate clause depends on a main clause for its meaning. It is usually introduced by a word like *who, which, that, when, where, because, if, although, while or before*. Often, though, *who, which* and *that* can be left out: *In a panic, she ripped up the letter he had written.**

Sentence building

Sentences come in all shapes and sizes. They can be:

a) **simple**, with only one subject. For example: *The girl wrote a story*.

b) simple, but with adjectives, adverbs and phrases added: *The little girl quickly wrote a funny story about a seahorse*.

c) **compound****, with subordinate clauses and extra main clauses: *The little girl took out her pen, and quickly wrote a funny story about a seahorse which swam across the Atlantic and then drowned in a puddle*.

Keep your sentences short, so that they are absolutely clear. Long, complicated sentences can sound clumsy.

--- **Sentence splitting** ---

The two articles below are each made up of one long, clumsy sentence. Break them both into two by taking out a comma and a conjunction and adding a period and a capital letter.

The **Lengthy Express**

BAGGED

Longville mayoress Mrs. Ponsonby-Smythe was in high spirits on Saturday, as she opened the church fête which Longville has been organizing for the past three weeks, but she refused to comment on the incident last week in which local woman Cora Redhanded attacked her with a purse, accusing her of stealing a bag of flour from her grocery store.

COUCH POTATO KIDS

Children are much less healthy these days, because they spend so much time sitting like couch potatoes in front of the television or playing computer games while they stuff their faces with chips and soda pop, and they don't get much exercise either, because they go everywhere by car or by public transportation, instead of walking.

*There is more about this on page 82.
**The word "compound" means "made up of several parts".

Clause spotting

Decide whether each group of words below is a main clause, a subordinate clause or a phrase. Put one of each type together to make four sentences, then arrange these into a short story, beginning *In the house next door ...*

In the house next door

in a fast car

which had incredibly long legs.

in a panic

One day he let it out

which squashed the poor stick insect.

while Mrs. Kettani was in her yard.

because she was terrified of large insects.

They arrived

She phoned the police

my friend kept a stick insect

in the street

Sentence stretch

Add an adjective, an adverb and a subordinate clause from the lists below to each of these sentences. (Put the adverb just in front of the verb, and the subordinate clause at the end.)

1   The monkey ate six bananas.

2   She eats at the restaurant.

3   He drove the car into a ditch.

4   Joanna walked up to the horse.

Adjectives: hungry, young, new, Chinese.

Adverbs: stupidly, slowly, greedily, often.

Subordinate clauses:
where her brother is a waiter.
which had thrown her off its back.
when the zookeeper had gone.
because he was fiddling with the radio.

an/a

an usually goes in front of:

a) words that begin with a vowel (*a, e, i, o* or *u*)
   egg, apple

b) words beginning with a letter such as *h* when it sounds like a vowel
   hour, heir

c) single letters (often in sets of initials) that sound like vowels
   SOS (*S* is said as "ess")
   MP (*M* is said as "em")

a usually goes in front of:

a) words that begin with a consonant (a letter that is not a vowel)
   door, book, clock

b) words beginning with vowels that sound like consonants
   university, European (both begin with "yuh" sounds)
   one-way street begins with a "wuh" sound)

Add either *an* or *a* to each of these nine sentences:

1   He gave me ... used railway ticket.
2   Jill said she had seen ... UFO.
3   They gave her ... X-ray and said she'd be fine.
4   From his window he has ... incredible view over New York.
5   This is ... one-way street.
6   Sometimes, a friend can turn into ... enemy.
7   It was such ... hot day.
8   It was ... honest answer.
9   He has ... older brother.

73

On these two pages you can find some useful hints on how to arrange words so that your sentences are as clear as possible.

Keeping together

Words that are connected to each other should always be kept together in a sentence. Here are two rules to help you with this:

1 Try to keep the subject and the verb as close together as possible, especially in long sentences. For example: _Jim_ _read_ the letter one last time, while Emma went to the phone and called the police.

The meaning can be unclear if the subject and the verb are far apart: _Jim_, while Emma went to the phone and called the police, _read_ the letter one last time.

2 Phrases and subordinate clauses should go as near as possible to the words they refer to.

If you put them in the wrong place, your sentence may sound very strange. For example: _The farmer rounded up the sheep that had run away_ <u>_with the sheepdog's help._</u>

Moving the phrase _with the sheepdog's help_ nearer to _the farmer_ makes the meaning clear: <u>_With the sheepdog's help, the farmer_</u> _rounded up the sheep that had run away._

Shifting adverbs

Certain adverbs, like _only_ and _just_, give sentences a slightly different meaning, depending on their position. You should normally put them in front of what they refer to, as shown here:

I told <u>only</u> Christopher that I had won second prize. (Christopher was the only person I told.)

I <u>only</u> told Christopher that I had won second prize. (It was the only thing I told him.)

I told Christopher that I had <u>only</u> won second prize. (I told him I had only won second prize, not first.)

Split infinitives

The **infinitive** of a verb (_to_ plus the verb, as in _to go, to work, to drive_) is its most basic form. You should avoid breaking up (or splitting) the two parts of the infinitive, particularly if you are writing formally or any time it sounds awkward. Thus, _to boldly go_ would be better phrased as _to go boldly_ or _boldly to go_.

Splitting up

Sarah's family are going away for the week. Spot the split infinitives in the notes they have left, then move the words that are splitting them to the end of the sentences.

You can finish all the food in the freezer, except for the chocolate cake I made for Dad's birthday, and the leg of lamb, which I'd like you to please take out on Saturday. Also, before Mr. Hopkins drops by on Wednesday, I'd like you to thoroughly vacuum the sitting room.

Before you go out, remember to carefully double-lock the door.

Please don't forget to put Bingo out before you go to bed. You need to every night feed my goldfish.

Could you remember to regularly water the tomatoes? By the way, I told Mary you'd try to quickly drop in on her.

SEE YOU ON SATURDAY – WE'RE GOING TO IF POSSIBLE TRY TO GET THE AFTERNOON TRAIN. PERHAPS YOU COULD PICK US UP FROM THE STATION IF WE GIVE YOU A CALL?

Picture puzzlers

Next to each pair of pictures below, there is a short sentence, and one phrase or clause (in yellow). Make two new sentences (one to match each picture) by inserting this phrase or clause in two different places in the sentence*.

1 The girl gave the envelope to the man.
with the dog

2 The man beat his rival.
who was wearing blue

3 The plant was in the corner of the room.
with the yellow flowers

4 Jane rested her foot on the top rung of the ladder.
which was shaking

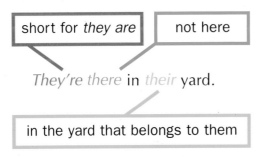

Adverb adding

Write out sentence 1 three times, putting the adverb *just* in a different place each time, so that the sentences have the meanings given in A, B and C.

Then do the same with sentence 2, using the adverb *only*.

Sentence 1: He's told me I will have to take it easy for a few days.
A He told me a minute ago.
B The only thing I have to do is take it easy.
C I have to take it easy, but only for a few days.

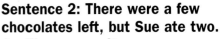

Sentence 2: There were a few chocolates left, but Sue ate two.
A There weren't many chocolates, but Sue took two anyway.
B There were some chocolates left, but Sue only took two.
C There were some chocolates left, but Sue was the only person who took two.

their/they're/there

Because they sound the same, it is easy to get *their, they're* and *there* mixed up. Here you can see the different meanings of these words:

| short for *they are* | | not here |

They're there in *their* yard.

| in the yard that belongs to them |

There is also used with *to be* to say things like *there is* (or *there's*) and *there are*.

For sentences 1 to 6, which word or group of words in brackets fits the gap?

1 There ... in a netball team.
(daughter is/all/are seven people)
2 Their ... outside.
(are two men/dog is/waiting)
3 They're ... in the swimming pool.
(still/dog is/we were)
4 Their ... way.
(lawyer is on his/is a tree in the/on their)
5 Isn't she there ...?
(new teacher/anymore)
6 They're ... on vacation.
(friend is/were two of us/away)

*You may need to add commas to make the meaning clear. See page 82.

Simple agreements

Always make sure that the subject agrees with (matches) the verb. Here you can see what this means:

singular subject	verb must be singular

Sarah is out,
but *the twins are* upstairs.

plural subject	verb must be plural

Tricky cases

Sometimes it is difficult to know whether to use a singular or plural verb with the subject. Here are some hints to help you:

1 The words *anyone, everyone, no one* and *each* are always followed by a singular verb. For example: *Everyone is asleep*.

The words *many, both, (a) few* and *several* are always followed by a plural verb. For example: *Several are missing*.

2 When the subject is two words joined by *and* (as in *Annie and her friend*), you use a plural verb: *Here come Annie and her friend*.

3 When the subject is a group of words, such as *members of the gang*, the verb must agree with the actual word it relates to:

These members of the gang are the toughest.

verb relates to this word (the *members* are the toughest, not the *gang*)	verb is plural to match *members*

4 Singular words which name groups of people (like *family, team* or *school*) can be used with either singular or plural verbs.

To talk about the group as a whole, you normally use a singular verb: *Each team has three turns*. To talk about it as a group of members, you can use a plural verb: *The team were excited about the match*.

Island mission

Agent Craxitall is on the trail of the notorious criminal, Ivor Cunningplan. He has discovered some pieces of the torn-up instructions for Ivor's latest mission. Fit them together to find out what Ivor has to do and where he is heading.

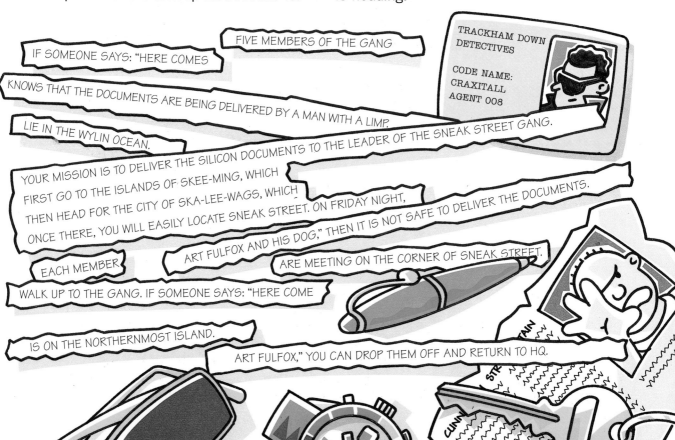

FIVE MEMBERS OF THE GANG

IF SOMEONE SAYS: "HERE COMES

TRACKHAM DOWN DETECTIVES
CODE NAME: CRAXITALL AGENT 008

KNOWS THAT THE DOCUMENTS ARE BEING DELIVERED BY A MAN WITH A LIMP.

LIE IN THE WYLIN OCEAN.

YOUR MISSION IS TO DELIVER THE SILICON DOCUMENTS TO THE LEADER OF THE SNEAK STREET GANG.

FIRST GO TO THE ISLANDS OF SKEE-MING, WHICH

THEN HEAD FOR THE CITY OF SKA-LEE-WAGS, WHICH

ONCE THERE, YOU WILL EASILY LOCATE SNEAK STREET. ON FRIDAY NIGHT,

THEN IT IS NOT SAFE TO DELIVER THE DOCUMENTS.

EACH MEMBER

ART FULFOX AND HIS DOG," THEN

ARE MEETING ON THE CORNER OF SNEAK STREET.

WALK UP TO THE GANG. IF SOMEONE SAYS: "HERE COME

IS ON THE NORTHERNMOST ISLAND.

ART FULFOX," YOU CAN DROP THEM OFF AND RETURN TO HQ.

Beach breaks

In this game, each white space shows the first half of a sentence. Starting at the blue arrow, move around from space to space, following the direction of the footprint containing the matching half sentence. You must go through all the white spaces before taking a red exit. Which exit, A to G, will you take?

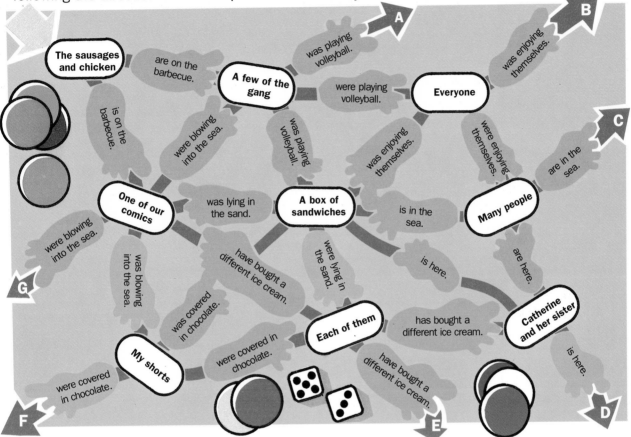

off/of

Off is nearly always connected to a verb. It can be a preposition (*They dropped it off the bridge*) or part of a verb (*They got off at the bus stop*).

Of is normally used after adjectives (as in *afraid of*), or after words that show quantity or numbers of things (as in *a few of, some of, a piece of, lots of*).

Of is sometimes used with a verb. In these cases, it often means *about* (for example, *to dream of, to think of*).

Which of these sentences is missing *off*, and which is missing *of*?

1 He is very proud ... his polar bear costume.
2 Kathy stopped ... in Zambia on her way to Swaziland.
3 Her brother reminds me ... a chimpanzee.
4 Most ... the chocolate fudge cake had already been eaten.
5 As she was getting ... the train, she saw the man.
6 Vicky has always been terrified ... cats.
7 The plane took ... late.

Fill the gaps

Fit one of the yellow words below into each sentence.

1 There ... layers of dust on the piano.
2 "Here ... Ann and Graham!" she shrieked, pointing across the street.
3 A little bit of money ... a long way.
4 When we got back, there ... a bucketful of tomatoes on the doorstep.
5 Most motorcycles are cheaper than cars and ... much faster.
6 Success ... more important to him than happiness.

is was go were are goes

77

Verbs have different forms for talking about the past, the present and the future. For example:

I worked, I am working, I will work. These different verb forms are called **tenses**.

Tenses Here you can see the main tenses. The examples, using the verb *to wait*, show how they are formed for most verbs.

PAST			PRESENT	FUTURE
past perfect	past simple*	present perfect	present simple*	future
had waited	*waited*	*have/has waited*	*wait/waits*	*shall/will wait*

For many common verbs, the past tenses are irregular (not formed in the way shown here). There is a list of common irregular verbs on page 16.

Many of these tenses also have **progressive** forms, such as the present continuous (I *am waiting*), and past continuous (I *was waiting*). These are normally used for something that is, was or will already be happening at a particular time.

There are other ways of talking about the future. For example, to talk about plans or things you intend to do, you can use *going to* with the verb (as in *Tomorrow I am going to write to my parents*).

Showing order

To talk about several things that happened at different times, you show the order they happened in by using different tenses. For example, when you use the past simple to talk about things that happened in the past, you can use the past perfect to show an action that took place even further back in time:

happened second	**happened first (a while ago)**

He *walked up* to the man who *had won*, and as he *handed* him the gleaming gold medal, he *said*, "Soon you *will be* famous."

both happened third (just after what happened second)	**will happen fourth**

When talking about a set of events, be careful not to jump from one tense to another (unless you are talking about things that happened at different times). Look at the example below.

She rushed downstairs, opened the door and <u>picks</u> up the package which the mailman had delivered. — **This should say <u>picked</u>.**

 like/as

You use *like* and *as* to compare things. Like goes in front of a noun or a pronoun. For example: *She is <u>like</u> her father.*

As goes in front of a clause (which has a subject and a verb). For example: *Everything was just <u>as</u> he had left it.*

As is also used in many other expressions which compare things in some way: <u>as</u> if, <u>as</u> good as, <u>as</u> usual, <u>as</u> before.

Make six sentences by joining a first half (on the left) with a second half (on the right), using *like*, *as* or *as if*.

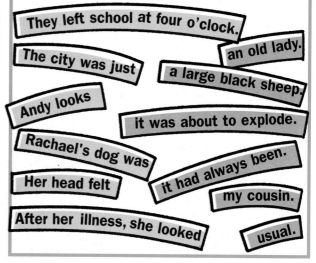

They left school at four o'clock.

The city was just

an old lady.

a large black sheep.

Andy looks

it was about to explode.

Rachael's dog was

it had always been.

Her head felt

my cousin.

After her illness, she looked

usual.

*In negative sentences (ones that use *not*) and in questions, use *did* with the past simple (*Did I wait?*) and *do/does* with the present simple (*He does not wait*).

Tense trippers

Louise has kept a diary of the cycling trip she went on with some friends, but she has put twelve verbs in the wrong tense. Can you correct her mistakes?

Monday
Just before lunch Stuart got a flat tire. No one had a flat tire repair kit, so we have to walk miles to the nearest town. When we finally got there, someone directed us to a bike shop, so we go all the way there and then find it was closed.

Tuesday
The day went well until we get caught behind a herd of sheep on a narrow lane. It took us two hours to get past them, so by the time we got to the youth hostel, it's completely full.

Wednesday
Stopped for lunch in a little village. Left our bikes by the church, went to a café, and when we come out, Sheila's bike has disappeared. Then suddenly we spotted the local priest riding the missing bike, so we flag him down and he explained everything. The poor priest sold his own bike a year ago, but he keeps forgetting, so every time he sees a black bike he thought it's his.

Thursday
Arrived at the station to get the train home. We loaded our bikes on board and then go for coffee while we are waiting. Suddenly, Stuart noticed that the train was leaving! We put our bikes on the wrong one!

Which is which?

Copy the list of verbs below. Then decide which tenses they are in, and underline each one as shown here:

past perfect
past simple
present perfect
present simple
future

have crashed
smiled
had promised
sit
had visited
will understand
did not arrive
buys
has spotted
will drive
invaded
sing
had painted

Getting snappy

Louise wanted to arrange her photos in the order in which they were taken, but she has mixed them up.

For each caption (A, B, C and D), write out the numbers of the photos in the order she should arrange them.

A At a local market, we met the boy who had fixed Stuart's bike, so we all went to the fair together.

B Every morning, fishermen in this village sell fresh fish that they have caught from their boats. By lunchtime, they will have none left.

C After we'd spotted the priest riding the bike Sheila had left outside the church, we all went for coffee together.

D On Tuesday, we had a picnic, and then went for a swim in a little cove we'd read about the night before.

79

Hints

These hints will help you decide which tenses to use in long sentences:

1 When the verb in the main clause is in the past tense (as in *I was mad*), the verbs in the subordinate clauses usually go into a past tense as well (*I was mad because he had not locked the door*).

2 When the verb in the main clause is in the future (*We will go*), or has a future meaning, verbs in the subordinate clauses usually go into the present (*We will go when he arrives*).

Which past tense?

You use the **past simple** to talk about something that happened at a particular time (as in *She arrived yesterday*).

You use the **present perfect** when it is not important to know exactly when something happened (*I have been to Egypt*), or when something is still going on (*I have lived here for two years*).

The present perfect is made using *has* or *have* and the **past participle**. For most verbs, the past participle is exactly like the past simple (*I called, I have called*).

The past participle is also used with *had* to form the **past perfect** (*I had called*). There is more about forming tenses on page 78.

Irregulars

Some common verbs have past simples and past participles that are **irregular**. This means they are not formed in the usual way (by adding *ed*). Here you can see a few tricky ones:

verb	past simple	past participle
to be	*was/were**	*been*
to begin	*began*	*begun*
to break	*broke*	*broken*
to do	*did*	*done*
to drink	*drank*	*drunk*
to eat	*ate*	*eaten*
to forget	*forgot*	*forgotten*
to give	*gave*	*given*
to go	*went*	*gone/been***
to run	*ran*	*run*
to sing	*sang*	*sung*
to swim	*swam*	*swum*
to take	*took*	*taken*

Can you think of any more verbs that have irregular past simples or past participles? You will need to know some others to do all the puzzles on these pages.

─────── **Lost for words** ───────

Which word from the yellow list below fits which speech bubble?

I have ... too much ice cream.

I ... a lot of ice cream when I was in Italy.

I have just ... my sister's sunglasses.

Last week I ... Mr. Bailey's window.

I ... in the bathtub this morning.

I have just ... across the lake.

I have ... all my homework.

I ... across it yesterday.

Nicky ... hers last week.

broke/broken/
swum/swam/
eaten/ate/
sang/done/did

*Use *was* with *I, he, she* and *it,* and *were* with *you, we* and *they.*
**Use *gone* when the subject is still away, and *been* when they have already returned.

Andrew's desk

Picture A shows what was on Andrew's desk one morning, and picture B shows what was there in the evening. Choosing verbs from the list below, write four sentences (beginning each one *He has ...*) to show what Andrew has done at his desk during the day.

Then rewrite these sentences, using the past simple. Begin each one *In the afternoon, ...*

to blow out, to break, to eat, to write

Tense trouble

Spot which verb is in the wrong tense in each of the sentences below.

1 They will have to pick up the house before their parents will get back.

2 Oliver had just finished writing when the examiner tells them to put down their pens.

3 Lots of people visit the exhibition when it opens next month.

4 I was furious because the train has been late.

5 She has been to Hong Kong last year.

6 They lived in New York for six years, and have no plans to move away.

can/may/might

Here you can see when to use *can*, *may* and *might*:

	can	may	might
1 Talking about something that is possible	use *can* to talk about something that you are able to do: *I can swim.*	use *may* for something that is possible and quite likely: *I may go for a swim.*	use *might* for something that is possible but not so likely: *I might go for a swim.*
2 Asking for permission	To ask permission or to give it, you can use *can* or *may*. *May* is more grammatically correct though, so you should use it in formal situations: *May I go home?* or *You may leave.* Use *can* in less formal situations: *Can I have a cookie?* or *You can have two chocolates.*		*might* is sometimes used in very formal situations: *Might I ask a question?*
3 Giving permission			never use *might*

Decide which word, *may*, *might* or *can* should fill the gaps in these sentences:

1 I am very glad that Jenny ... speak French.
2 You ... spend as much money as you like.
3 ... I borrow a pencil? (talking to a friend)
4 ... I phone my parents? (talking to someone you don't know)
5 I ... go and see a movie this afternoon, if it keeps on raining.

*Could is often used instead of can to ask for permission. It is less direct (and more polite) than can.

Which, that, who, whom and *whose* are called **relative pronouns**. They usually introduce clauses which tell you more about a noun. For example: There are those *awful people who live at number 6*.

Different clauses

Relative pronouns work in different ways, depending on whether they are introducing a restrictive or a non-restrictive clause.

An **restrictive clause** spells out who or what the noun is, as in *There is the dog which bit my rabbit*.

A **non-restrictive clause** simply tells you more about a noun whose identity is already clear. Think of it as the part of the sentence that could go in parentheses. For example: *Mr. Parker's dog, which bit my rabbit, has just attacked the milkman*.

When speaking, you do not often use non-identifying clauses. They are always split off from the rest of the sentence by commas, but restrictive clauses are not.

Relative pronouns

Here you can see which relative pronoun to use, depending on whether you are talking about a person or a thing*:

RESTRICTIVE CLAUSES

for people	who (or whom)/that
for things	which/that

1 *That* can often replace *who* or *which* (as in the man that stole the bananas).
2 You can often leave out the relative pronoun altogether: *That is the dog (which) I rescued.*

NON-RESTRICTIVE CLAUSES

for people	who (or whom)
for things	which

1 You cannot use *that* instead of *who* or *which*.
2 You cannot leave out the relative pronoun.

Whom, whose

Whom can stand for a person, if that person is the object** of the clause (as in *That is the doctor whom I saw*). In spoken English, it is normally replaced with *who* or *that*.

Whose stands for someone to whom something belongs (*The man whose car I had hit chased me*).

Prepositions

After a preposition (see page 70), you use *whom* instead of *who*, and *which* instead of *that*. For example: *the man to whom I gave my ticket*. It is often easier, though, to turn the clause around and leave out the relative pronoun: *the man I gave my ticket to*.

—**Identity crisis**—

Rewrite the sentences below, removing any non-restrictive clauses.

1 **The fridge is full of bacon, which I eat every day.**
2 **The ring which he gave me was far too big.**
3 **The policeman who drove them home was very friendly.**
4 **My brother, who is a vet, is getting married.**
5 **The boat, which was found by a diver, had been underwater for thirty years.**

—**Who or *whom*?**—

Write out these sentences, completing two with *who* and two with *whom*.

1 **The friend with ... I went to Egypt has sent me a letter.**
2 **The people ... took the other path got there first.**
3 **Valerie, ... has just come back from Mexico, speaks fluent Spanish.**
4 **This is Jo, ... I met on a bus.**

*For an animal, depending on how you think of it, you can either follow the pattern for people or for things.
**Remember, the subject does the action and the object has the action done to it.

Murder at Snoot Towers

Read this report on the murder of Lord Snoot, and decide which relative pronoun (below) should go in each space. Then use the plan of Snoot Towers to identify the most likely murderer.

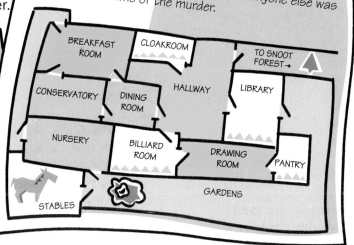

Lord Snoot's body, ..1.. was found in the conservatory, was identified by his widow. Lady Snoot, ..2.. will inherit several million pounds from her husband, was in the drawing room with the gardener at the time of the murder, looking at designs for a sunken garden ..3.. she wanted installed. Hugo Batty, ..4.. knew the truth about Snoot's business affairs, and to ..5.. Snoot had just given ten thousand dollars, was working in the library. Will Snoot, ..6.. fiancée was lunching with his sister in the dining room (both women are eliminated from the inquiry), was shooting grouse in Snoot Forest. Lord Snoot had earlier forbidden him to marry his fiancée. The cook and the butler were in the pantry, ..7.. can only be reached from the drawing room. They said they heard Lord Snoot's cousin, Earl Toffeenose, talking in the billiard room with the nanny, ..8.. Snoot had just fired. Nobody passed through any of the rooms ..9.. anyone else was in around the time of the murder.

that/which
whom
who
which
whose
which
whom/that
that
who

BREAKFAST ROOM | **CLOAKROOM** | **TO SNOOT FOREST→**
CONSERVATORY | **DINING ROOM** | **HALLWAY** | **LIBRARY**
NURSERY | **BILLIARD ROOM** | **DRAWING ROOM** | **PANTRY**
STABLES | **GARDENS**

of/'ve

In speech, *have* is often shortened to *'ve* after *should, would, may, must, might* and so on. For example: *You should've gone.**

Be careful not to confuse *'ve* with *of*, which sounds very similar. Never use *of* instead of *have* with the words listed above.

Complete these pieces of conversation with *should've, would've, could've* and *must've*. (Use each once only.)

1 "She ... decided not to take her car, because I saw it parked in our street this morning."
2 "You really ... gone to the party: it was great fun."
3 "We ... driven a bit faster, but not much, as the roads are very wet."
4 "If it hadn't been raining, I ... come."

Who's who and what's what?

Look at the pictures, then decide which clause from the list on the right fits which sentence best. (Use each once only.)

1 The girl ... is near the boat.
2 The dog ... has black paws.
3 The ice cream ... is chocolate and vanilla.
4 The boy ... has red hair.
5 The cow ... has black ears.
6 The dog ... is near the boat.
7 The baby ... has a pink hat.
8 The man ... has a red sweater.

THE POLICEMAN IS CHASING
WHICH IS SWIMMING
WHICH THE BOY IS HOLDING
WHICH IS RUNNING
WHO IS SWIMMING
WHOM THE POLICEMAN IS CHASING
WHO IS RUNNING
THE WOMAN IS HOLDING

*When writing, you should normally use *have*, not *'ve.*

Comparatives and superlatives

Comparatives and superlatives are special forms of adjectives that are used for comparing things.

You use a **comparative** (such as *taller, more intelligent*) to compare people or things with each other. For example: *Simon is <u>taller</u> than Andrew and Tim.*

You use a **superlative** (such as *the tallest, the most intelligent*) to show that one thing stands out above all the rest. For example: *Simon is <u>the tallest</u> in the class.*

Different forms

Most comparatives are made either by adding *er* to the adjective, or putting *more* in front of it. Most superlatives are made by adding *est* or putting *the most* in front.

The form you use depends on how many syllables the adjective has. A **syllable** is part of a word that contains a vowel sound. For example, *lazy* has two syllables containing the vowel sounds "ay" and "ee".

Here are some general rules on which form to use. Examples are shown in blue:

ADJECTIVE	COMPARATIVE	SUPERLATIVE
one-syllable adjective* *hard*	*-er* *harder*	*the -est* *the hardest*
one-syllable adjective ending in *e* *white*	*-r* *whiter*	*the -st* *the whitest*
adjective with two or more syllables *careful*	*more ...* *more careful*	*the most ...* *the most careful*
two-syllable adjective ending in *y* *funny*	*-er (and change y to i)* *funnier*	*the -est (and change y to i)* *the funniest*

The important thing to remember is that you either add *er* (or *est*) OR use *more* (or *the most*). Never do both.

Irregulars Here are some common adjectives which have irregular comparatives and superlatives:

ADJECTIVE	COMPARATIVE	SUPERLATIVE
good	*better*	*the best*
bad	*worse*	*the worst*
much/many	*more*	*the most*
little	*less*	*the least*

Adverbs, I/me

Adverbs also have comparative and superlative forms. These work just as for adjectives, except that for most long adverbs ending in y, you use *more/the most* instead of adding *er/est*.

It is common to use *me, him, her, us* and *them* after a comparative with *than* (as in *He is older than <u>me</u>*). In formal situations, though, people sometimes use *I, he, she, we* and *they* (*He is older than I*).

Comparing climates

Look at these charts of the temperature and total rainfall for two cities through the year. Then write out the sentences below, adding comparatives of *hot, cold* (for 1 and 2), *wet* and *dry* (for 3 and 4).

1 **In August, Weatherchester is ... than Seasonbury.**
2 **In January, Weatherchester is ... than Seasonbury.**
3 **In March, Seasonbury is ... than Weatherchester.**
4 **In September, Seasonbury is ... than Weatherchester.**

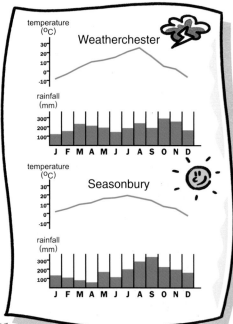

84 *For adjectives ending in *y* (such as *dry*), you change *y* to *i* (*drier, the driest*). For those ending in one vowel and one consonant (such as *hot*), you double the consonant (*hotter, the hottest*).

Character questionnaire

Jon and Tessa have done a magazine quiz, each of them putting their initial by the answer they have chosen. Based on their answers, and making comparatives from the adjectives on the list, write six sentences comparing Jon and Tessa. For example: *Jon is taller than Tessa.*

NOSY SELFISH LAZY FRIENDLY PATIENT CAREFUL

Quiz

1 You have been waiting for a bus for half an hour. You:
a) wait patiently, feeling glad you are not in a hurry. **J**
b) pace up and down, looking at your watch. **T**
c) decide to walk - the exercise will do you good.

2 Arriving home, you realize you have forgotten to mail an urgent letter for your mother. You:
a) pretend to have forgotten all about it until it is too late. **J**
b) ask your brother to mail it on his way to football practice.
c) go straight out to mail it before you forget again. **T**

3 There is a new girl in your class, and at lunchtime you notice her sitting on her own. You:
a) ask her to come and join you and your friends. **T**
b) make a point of talking to her later on.
c) ignore her. **J**

4 You are walking a friend's dog in the countryside. You:
a) put it on a leash every time you see a road ahead. **J**
b) keep an eye on it whenever you are on a road.
c) let it wander ahead - after all, the roads are very quiet. **T**

5 You hear your sister on the phone and she is clearly upset. You:
a) strain your ears to listen in. **T**
b) hum loudly, so you can't hear anything. **J**
c) listen in, then ask her later on what was wrong.

6 For your birthday you are given a small box of chocolates. You:
a) guzzle them in your room rather than share them. **J**
b) offer them around once, then eat the rest yourself.
c) offer them to all your friends, leaving none for yourself. **T**

quite/quiet

People often confuse these words. *Quite* is an adverb that either means "very" (as in *I'm quite tired*), or "completely" (*I'm quite lost*). *Quiet* is an adjective that means the opposite of "noisy"/"loud".

Passed and *past* are also confusing. *Passed* can only be used as a verb (as in *He passed the salt*). *Past* can be used as an adjective (*the past year*), a noun (*He lives in the past*), a preposition (*She ran past me*) or an adverb (*A gull flew past*).

Write these sentences out, adding *quite, quiet, passed* or *past.*

1 You look ... washed out.
2 As Stefan walked ..., he noticed the man's gun.
3 It is very ... without Diane and Vicky.
4 Veronica was so happy when she ... her test.
5 In the ... week, I have lost two umbrellas.
6 I have always found math ... hard.

Moped mania

Sally is not sure which moped to buy. Using the table on the right, and the adjectives *wide, long, expensive, fast* and *heavy*, write five sentences to compare the Superwhizz and the Pipsqueak.

Then do the same for the Stumbly and the Featherzoom, and for the Pipsqueak and the Thriftyshift.

Sally can only spend $4000, and the space in her garage is 3 x 10 feet. Which is the fastest moped she can buy?

Moped	Width (feet)	Length (feet)	Price ($)	Top speed (miles per hour)	Weight (lbs)
Superwhizz	3	9.5	4500	65	95
Pipsqueak	2	8	3800	50	75
Stumbly	3.5	9.5	3000	40	80
Featherzoom	3	11	3400	60	65
Thriftyshift	2.5	10	2000	45	70

Conditional sentences are used to talk about things that can only happen under certain conditions*. For example: *If he said he was sorry, I would forgive him.*

There are three main types. They are made up of two clauses, each in a different tense, one of which is introduced by *if*. Most contain a verb in the **conditional** (such as *would go*) or **conditional perfect** (*would have gone*).

Type 1

if clause in present tense	other clause in future tense

"If I win an Olympic medal,
I will give all the prize money to charity."

This type is used to talk about something that is likely to happen. In the example, the person speaking has a good chance of winning an Olympic medal.

Type 2

if clause in past tense	other clause in conditional

"If I won an Olympic medal,
I would give all the prize money to charity."

This type is used to talk about something that is unlikely to happen. In the example, the person speaking is just imagining what it would be like to win an Olympic medal.

Type 3

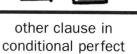

if clause in past perfect	other clause in conditional perfect

"If I had won an Olympic medal,
I would have given all the prize money to charity."

This type is used to imagine what would have been possible if things had turned out differently. In the example, the person speaking entered the Olympics, but did not win a medal.

Always remember that the conditional perfect does not go in the *if* clause. This means it is wrong to say things like *if I'd have had.*

Was/were, should In formal
situations, you should use *were*** instead of *was*** after *if*. This is especially true when you are giving advice. For example: *If I __were__ you, I wouldn't do that.*
   You can use *should* instead of *would* when the subject is *I* or *we*. For example: *If I were you, I __should__ stay at home.*

---

in/into

To show that something moves from one place to another, use *into*, especially after the verbs *go, come, walk* and *run*. For example: *Ellie ran __into__ the room.*
   To show that something stays in the same place, use *in* (*It is __in__ the corner*).
   Lots of verbs can be used with either *in* or *into*, but stick to the rules given above and you will always be right.

Add *in* or *into* to each of these sentences:

1   **He could see a girl diving ... the pool.**
2   **Elaine hurried ... her bedroom.**
3   **The train had been waiting ... the tunnel for more than half an hour.**
4   **We went ... the garden to look for worms.**
5   **I lay ... the bathtub for forty minutes today.**

---

*When you talk about facts, rather than conditions, you don't need the conditional tense. For example: *If you heat ice, it melts.*
**These are forms of the verb *to be.*

Split conditionals

Here you can see six sentences which have each been split in two. Put them back together again and match each sentence with the correct picture.

they would not have died.

If I water the plants,

I will bite her.

I would have won.

I will win.

If she had pulled my ear,

I would have bitten her.

If she pulls my ear,

If I had watered the plants,

they will not die.

If I run faster,

If I had run faster,

Dear Maisie

Look at this magazine problem page. Can you replace each number with the correct form of one of the verbs shown here?

to think/to pass/to stop/to be/ to have to/to speak/to eat

HELP!

Dear Maisie,
I failed all my finals again this semester, and my teacher says that if I don't work harder, I ..1.. leave the school. But I just can't concentrate.

Switch the TV off and put those magazines away. If you ..2.. your exams the first time, you wouldn't have had these problems.

Dear Maisie,
I want to become a vegetarian, but my mother says if I ..3.. eating meat I will be sick.

Your mother is right to be concerned, but if you ..4.. lots of protein foods you will not be ill.

Dear Maisie,
I have an enormous pimple on the end of my nose. I've tried everything, but I just can't get rid of it.

If I ..5.. you, I would try some Wondersqueeze cream. It never fails!

Dear Maisie,
I want to join a tennis club, but I'm very shy. If anyone ..6.. to me, I would turn bright red and start shaking.

In that case, you should definitely join a tennis club. If you do turn red and start shaking, no one ..7.. it is odd: lots of people are very shy.

A wobbly welcome

Barry, the Boppa Breaks tourist guide, has written a welcome note for tourists arriving in Costa Boppa. He has circled a few mistakes that he has made, but is not sure how to correct them. Can you make the necessary corrections?

Hi folks! Welcome to Costa Boppa! This is the world's most remote island: if you (came) by boat it would have taken you thirty-nine hours to get here. But it's also the world's most happening hotspot: if you went to the Costa Brava you (will not find) wilder nightlife.

Costa Boppa is simply gorgeous. If you got up at four o'clock, you (would have seen) some amazing sunrises. If you (wanted) to explore the island a bit, your Boppa Breaks guide will be happy to arrange a bus tour and cultural extravaganza.

If you come on down to the Boppa Breaks karaoke evening tonight, we (would tell) you more about all the great entertainment lined up for you this week.

Well, that's it, folks. If you (will have) any questions, just buzz Larry, Carrie or me, Barry, at the Paradise Club.

To show what someone said, you can either use direct or reported speech. **Direct speech** is when you put the person's exact words in quotation marks ("..."). For example: *Lee said, "I am feeling very tired."*

Reported speech is when you describe what someone said. When you do this, you change the verb into the past tense, even if the information is still true. For example: *Lee said that he was feeling very tired.*

Reporting

To put something like *Ann said, "I cooked this yesterday"* into reported speech, you drop the quotation marks* and make these changes:

You usually add that.**	I and you often change to he or she.

Ann said *that she* *had cooked that the day before*.

The tense of the verbs changes.	Some expressions change.

Tenses

In reported speech, you move the tense of the verbs back into the past and change time expressions.

For example, Vicky says to Alice, "*Ian is taking his test today.*" If Alice wants to report to Debbie what Vicky has said, she should say: "*Vicky said that Ian was taking his test today.*" This applies even if Ian has not actually taken his test yet.

Here is a summary of how tenses change when verbs go into reported speech:

she ...	I said that she ...
smiles (present simple)	smiled (past simple)
is smiling (present continuous)	was smiling (past continuous)
has smiled, smiled, had smiled (present perfect, past simple, past perfect)	had smiled (past perfect)
will/would smile (future, conditional)	would smile (conditional)

In informal situations it is sometimes acceptable not to change the tense, when you report something that is still true (as in *Melissa said Canada is a great place to live*).

Expressions

Here you can see how some common expressions can change when they go into reported speech:

today	that day
yesterday	the day before
tomorrow	the next day
next (week)	the following (week)
last (week)/ a (week) ago	the (week) before
this (week)	that (week)
here	there
this/these	that/those

Questions and orders

To report a question (such as *Kate asked, "What are you doing?"*), you take the verb out of its question form, as well as making the usual changes. So you say *Kate asked what <u>I was doing</u>*, not *what <u>was I doing</u>*.

For questions that do not start with words like *what, where, when* or *why*, you add *if* or *whether*: *He asked <u>if</u> I was sick*.

When you report an order or piece of advice, you normally use the infinitive: *He told me <u>to go home</u>*.

As shown with these examples, with reported questions and orders, you cannot use *said* as the introducing verb. You normally use *asked* in front of a question, and *told, advised, commanded* or *warned* in front of an order.

──On the record──

Put these sentences into reported speech, following the guidelines given on this page.

1 **Liz said, "I ate Jo's chocolates yesterday."**
2 **Bobby said to us, "What did you do today?"**
3 **Carol said, "I am playing squash with my sister today."**
4 **Neil said, "Has Mandy borrowed my bike?"**
5 **The teacher said to us, "Never run across the street without looking both ways."**

88

*You also drop the colon (:) or comma (,) that comes in front of what is said.
**After common verbs like *say* and *tell,* you can leave *that* out: *Jo said he had cooked that the week before.*

to/too

To is normally a preposition. You use it to talk about movement from one place to another (as in *I am going to the store*) and time (*It is five to three*). You use it after certain adjectives (*I am responsible to the manager*) and verbs (*He looks forward to Mondays*). *To* also makes up the infinitive of a verb, as in *to dream*.

Too is an adverb. You use it with other adverbs or adjectives to talk about something that is excessive (more than needed). For example: *He drives too fast*. *Too* is often used with *much* or *many* (*There are too many people*). It can also mean "as well" (*Bob is a teacher, and Shirley is too*).

Write this postcard out, filling the gaps with *to* or *too*.

... Ellie,
Having a great time here in India. Yesterday we went ... the Taj Mahal, and tomorrow we are planning ... go on a pony-trek and visit some palaces ... . We are getting used ... the heat now, but at first it just seemed ... hot ... do anything. Eating far ... many curries and spending ... much money. Anyway, it's ten ... ten and time for me ... go ... bed. Looking forward ... seeing you next week.

Much love,
Rob

The Noah C. Parker Interview

Read Noah C. Parker's interview with the soap opera star, I. MacOoldood. Then use it to write down (in full sentences) the star's replies to the questions he was asked.

Noah's natter

Mac told me that he had first decided to be a soap opera star at the age of three. He also told me that he was working on a new soap opera called Suds and Scandal, all about life at a laundromat. He said that in his spare time he did a lot of yoga and also knitted his own sweaters. And his real personality? He said he was like all celebrities - the life and soul of parties and lots of fun. Is it true, though, that his best friend is his pet rat? Mac said he had hundreds of friends, but Reginald the rat was great because he never answered back. As for travel, Mac said that he hated foreign food and having to shout to make himself understood. And his ambitions? Mac said that one day he would be the most famous person in the world.

1 When did you decide you wanted to be a soap opera star?
2 What are you working on at the moment?
3 What do you do in your spare time?
4 How would you describe your personality?
5 Is it true that your best friend is your pet rat?
6 Do you like traveling?
7 What are your ambitions?

Drama in Drabsby

Look at this report from the Drabsby News, and the reporter's notes on three interviews he has done. Then decide how to fill the gaps in the report. (Follow the rules on reported speech on page 88.)

Drama in Drabsby

The world-famous painting Los Forreva has been snatched from Drabsby Museum by a gang of cunning crooks. Last week's theft was discovered by curator Ivor Topjob. He said that he ..1.. at the museum at quarter past nine, and that he ..2.. at once that Los Forreva ..3.. . Extraordinarily, there appears to be no sign of any break-in. Detective B. Wildered, investigating this mysterious case, said he ..4.. so baffled by a crime, but stressed that he ..5.. into every possibility. Caretaker Luke Safteritt, who said that he ..6.. the museum as usual at half past six ..7.., insists that it was all locked up. He said that he ..8.. a door or window of the museum unlocked in all his time ..9.. . However, Ivor Topjob said that he ..10.. a few questions to ask the caretaker ..11..

Caretaker: I left the museum at half past six yesterday, as usual, and the whole place was locked and bolted. In the thirty years that I have worked here, I have never left a single door or window unlocked.

Detective B. Wildered: I have never been so baffled by a crime. When I arrived at the museum there was no sign of a break-in, yet the caretaker swears that all the doors and windows were locked. I am looking into every possibility.

Curator: I arrived at the museum at about quarter past nine, opened up, and realized at once that Los Forreva had gone. There were no broken windows or doors, though: I will have a few questions to ask the caretaker today.

Negative niggles

A **negative sentence** contains a negative word such as *not*, *nobody*, *nothing* or *never*. Be careful not to use two negative words, as this makes a sentence positive. For example: *Nobody* did *nothing* means everybody did something. The correct negative sentence is *Nobody did anything*.

When you use *not* with the infinitive of a verb (such as *to run*), it must go in front of *to*. (Otherwise you would be splitting the infinitive; see page 74.) For example: *Try not to run*.

Pronoun problems

The pronouns *it* and *you* can be subjects or objects. The others are more tricky: you use *I, he, she, we* and *they* as subjects (as in *I smiled at Jo*), but *me, him, her, us* and *them* as objects (*Jo smiled at me*). These hints will help you know which to use:

1 Use object pronouns after a preposition: *Tom is working with me today*.

2 Use subject pronouns after *as* and *than* if they are followed by a verb. For example: *I am older than he is*. When there is no verb, it is common to use object pronouns: *I am older than him*. In formal situations, though, people might say: *I am older than he*.

3 When the subject or object is two words joined by *and*, make sure you use the correct pronoun. For example: *Maria and I* (subject) *are visiting Paul*, but *Paul is visiting Maria and me* (object).

Bothers with "be"

People often use the wrong form of *to be*. For example, they say *you was* instead of *you were*. Here are the right forms:

Present simple	Past simple
I am you/we/they are he/she/it is	I was* you/we/they were he/she/it was

Trouble with "them"

Never use *them* instead of *those* in front of a noun. You should say *Pass me those keys*, NOT *Pass me them keys*.

The Supertone chair

Get rid of the mistakes in this advertisement by replacing eight words with the ones listed on the yellow note (use each once only).

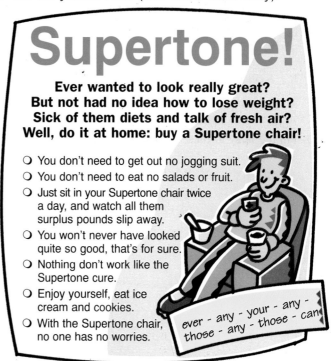

Supertone!

**Ever wanted to look really great?
But not had no idea how to lose weight?
Sick of them diets and talk of fresh air?
Well, do it at home: buy a Supertone chair!**

○ You don't need to get out no jogging suit.
○ You don't need to eat no salads or fruit.
○ Just sit in your Supertone chair twice a day, and watch all them surplus pounds slip away.
○ You won't never have looked quite so good, that's for sure.
○ Nothing don't work like the Supertone cure.
○ Enjoy yourself, eat ice cream and cookies.
○ With the Supertone chair, no one has no worries.

ever - any - your - any - those - any - those - can

Pronoun puzzler

Write out these sentences, adding one of the pronouns given in parentheses.

1 Someone has invited ... and his cousin to go to Japan. (he/him)
2 You know more about it than ... do. (I/me)
3 I hope Gary will dance with ... . (we/us)
4 Paula and ... are going out for lunch. (I/me)
5 Her brother is almost as tall as ... . (she/her)

A letter home

Write out Lucy's letter, correcting the seven mistakes she has made.

Dear Ben,
Thanks very much for the comics you sent me: they was really funny. My Dad and me went ice skating last week, and he kept falling over. I was desperately trying to not burst out laughing. My finals start next week, but I'm trying to not think about them. Otherwise I don't really have nothing to tell you. Don't forget to send me them photos you took when we was at the fair last week.
Lots of love,
Lucy

*After *if*, it is sometimes correct to say *I were*. For example: *If I were you, I would not do that*. There is more about this on page 86.

Page 67

Jumbled nouns

The unscrambled nouns are:
1 Paris (**Pisar**)   6 van (**nav**)
2 cleaners (**ranclees**)   7 dogs (**sodg**)
3 painting (**gnapinit**)   8 prison (**rosnip**)
4 policeman (**clamponie**) 9 tourists (**russitot**)
5 doors (**rodos**)

Give and take

A They had bought the **rusty** old car in **Bangkok**.
B Where is **Sarah** today?
C Outside the house stood a shiny **black bicycle**.
D I'm too **busy** to take the **dog** for a walk today.

Pages 68-69

Pronoun fillers

1	it	4	we	7	she
2	he	5	them	8	me
3	I	6	us	9	her

Identity parade

Verbs:	Nouns:	Words that can be either:
follow,	window,	scream,
undo,	desk,	study,
add,	shirt,	hope,
wander,	drawer,	fly,
write	girl	climb

1 My sister is hoping to **study** art at college.
2 We managed to **climb** up onto the ridge of the mountain.
3 Her only **hope** now is that the train is running late.
4 When the man jumped out from behind the door, she let out a loud **scream**.
5 Mark swatted the **fly** that kept buzzing around the room.

Sentence spinner

The five sentences you can find are:
I have won a bronze medal.
It was following the young girl.
We are catching an early plane.
They bought a black dog.
She knows the tall man.
It was following the young girl still makes sense when the object and subject are swapped over: *The young girl was following it.*

A sack of words

Nouns: postcard, song, Louise, computer, beauty
Verbs: will buy, to cry, is working, to dream, waited
Adjectives: unhappy, sunny, loud
Pronouns: she, we, they, you
Articles: an, the, a

affect/effect

Affect is a verb. *Effect* is usually a noun.
1 What is the **effect** of adding flour to water?
2 That movie was really good. There were lots of special **effects**.
3 I had a cold, but it didn't really **affect** me very badly.
4 Her illness had a very bad **effect** on her test results.
5 The weather can **affect** the way you feel.

Pages 70-71

Scrambled - after, between, across, into, under

1 My car was parked **between** the truck and the motorcycle.
2 They walked home **after** the party.
3 The dog jumped **into** the lake.
4 The prisoner ran as fast as he could **across** the bridge.
5 The money was hidden **under** the bed.

Sentence building

He couldn't remember her name, **although** he had met her before.
He forced the door open **and** crept quietly into the house.
Michelle rushed to the window and looked for the car, **but** it had already gone.
I can't play tennis today **because** my knee hurts.
She listened to music on her headphones **while** she was jogging.

Sentence parts

1 (The) / (dog) / (ran) / (into) / (the) / (road,) / (and) / (the) / (car) / (just) / (missed) / (it.)
2 (We) / (are having) / (a) / (big) / (party,) / (so) / (you) / (must come.)
3 (The) / (big) / (bear) / (escaped) / (from) / (the) / (zoo) / (and) / (was) / (never) / (seen) / (again.)
4 (The) / (dancers) / (were) / (so) / (shocked,) / (they) / (had to stop) / (the) / (show.)

borrow/lend; teach/learn

Fill the gap

1	muddy	6	creaky	11	cheerful
2	loud	7	lightly	12	merrily
3	quietly	8	faint	13	thankfully
4	empty	9	deeply		
5	heavily	10	suddenly		

Pages 72-73

Sentence splitting

Here you can see where you should have broken up the sentences (losing *but* and *and*):
... for the past three weeks. She refused to ...
... with chips and soda pop. They don't get ...

Clause spotting

Main clauses: She phoned the police/They arrived/my friend kept a stick insect/One day he let it out
Subordinate clauses: which squashed the poor stick insect/which had incredibly long legs/while Mrs. Kettani was in her yard/because she was terrified of large insects
Phrases: in a fast car/In the house next door/in a panic/in the street

In the house next door, my friend kept a stick insect which had incredibly long legs. One day he let it out in the street while Mrs. Kettani was in her yard. She phoned the police in a panic because she was terrified of large insects. They arrived in a fast car which squashed the poor stick insect.

Sentence stretch

Here are some examples of the most likely extended sentences.

1 The **hungry** monkey **greedily** ate six bananas **when the zookeeper had gone**.
2 She **often** eats at the **Chinese** restaurant **where her brother is a waiter**.
3 He **stupidly** drove the **new** car into a ditch, **because he was fiddling with the radio**.
4 Joanna **slowly** walked up to the **young** horse **which had thrown her off its back**.

an/a

1 He gave me **a** used railway ticket.
2 Jill said she had seen **a** UFO.
3 They gave her **an** X-ray and said she'd be fine.
4 From his window he has **an** incredible view over New York.
5 This is **a** one-way street.
6 Sometimes, a friend can turn into **an** enemy.
7 It was such **a** hot day.
8 It was **an** honest answer.
9 He has **an** older brother.

Pages 74-75

Splitting up

You can finish all the food in the freezer, except for the chocolate cake I made for Dad's birthday, and the leg of lamb, which I'd like you **to take out on Saturday, please**. Also, before Mr. Hopkins drops by on Wednesday, I'd like you **to vacuum the sitting room thoroughly**. Could you remember **to water the tomatoes regularly**? By the way, I told Mary you'd try **to drop in on her quickly**.
Before you go out, remember **to double-lock the door carefully**.
Please don't forget to put Bingo out before you go to bed. You need **to feed my goldfish every night**. See you on Saturday - we're going **to try to get the afternoon train if possible**. Perhaps you could pick us up from the station if we give you a call?

Picture puzzlers

The sentences that match the pictures on the left are:
1 The girl with the dog gave the envelope to the man.
2 The man who was wearing blue beat his rival.
3 The plant was in the corner of the room with the yellow flowers.
4 Jane rested her foot, which was shaking, on the top rung of the ladder.
The sentences that match the pictures on the right are:
1 The girl gave the envelope to the man with the dog.
2 The man beat his rival, who was wearing blue.
3 The plant with the yellow flowers was in the corner of the room.
4 Jane rested her foot on the top rung of the ladder, which was shaking.

Adverb adding

1A He's **just** told me I will have to take it easy for a few days.
1B He's told me I will **just** have to take it easy for a few days.
1C He's told me I will have to take it easy **just** for a few days or for **just** a few days.
2A There were **only** a few chocolates left, but Sue ate two.
2B There were a few chocolates left, but Sue **only** ate two.
2C There were a few chocolates left, but **only** Sue ate two.

their/they're/there

1 There **are seven people** in a netball team.
2 Their **dog is** outside.
3 They're **still** in the swimming pool.
4 Their **lawyer is on his** way.
5 Isn't she there **anymore**?
6 They're **away** on vacation.

Pages 76-77

Island mission

Here you can see what Ivor Cunningplan's instructions say when they are pieced together:
Your mission is to deliver the Silicon documents to the leader of the Sneak Street gang.
First go to the islands of Skee-ming, which lie in the Wylin Ocean. Then head for the city of Ska-lee-wags, which is on the northernmost island. Once there, you will easily locate Sneak Street.
On Friday night, five members of the gang are meeting on the corner of Sneak Street. Each member knows that the documents are being delivered by a man with a limp. Walk up to the gang. If someone says: "Here come Art Fulfox and his dog," then it is not safe to deliver the documents. If someone says: "Here comes Art Fulfox," you can drop them off and return to HQ.

Beach breaks

You will take exit C.
The matched-up sentences you will make are:
  The sausages and chicken are on the barbecue.
  A few of the gang were playing volleyball.
  Everyone was enjoying themselves.
  A box of sandwiches was lying in the sand.
  One of our comics was blowing into
  the sea.
  My shorts were covered in chocolate.
  Each of them has bought a different ice cream.
  Catherine and her sister are here.
  Many people are in the sea.

off/of

Sentences 1, 3, 4 and 6 are missing *of*.
Sentences 2, 5 and 7 are missing *off*.

Fill the gaps

1 There **were** layers of dust on the piano.
2 "Here **are** Ann and Graham!" she shrieked, pointing across the street.
3 A little bit of money **goes** a long way.
4 When we got back, there **was** a bucketful of tomatoes on the doorstep.
5 Most motorcycles are cheaper than cars and **go** much faster.
6 Success **is** more important to him than happiness.

Pages 78-79

like/as

They left school at four o'clock, **as** usual.
The city was just **as** it had always been.
Andy looks **like** my cousin.
Rachael's dog was **like** a large black sheep.
Her head felt **as if** it was about to explode.
After her illness, she looked **like** an old lady.

Tense trippers

Monday
Just before lunch Stuart got a flat tire. No one had a flat tire repair kit, so we **had** to walk miles to the nearest town. When we finally got there, someone directed us to a bike shop, so we **went** all the way there and then **found** it was closed.

Tuesday
The day went well until we **got** caught behind a herd of sheep on a narrow lane. It took us two hours to get past them, so by the time we got to the youth hostel, it **was** completely full.

Wednesday
Stopped for lunch in a little village. Left our bikes by the church, went to a café, and when we **came** out, Sheila's bike **had** disappeared. Then suddenly we spotted the local priest riding the missing bike, so we **flagged** him down and he explained everything. The poor priest sold his own bike a year ago, but he keeps forgetting, so every time he sees a black bike he **thinks** it's his.

Thursday
Arrived at the station to get the train home. We loaded our bikes on board and then **went** for coffee while we **were** waiting. Suddenly, Stuart noticed that the train was leaving! We **had put** OR We'**d put** our bikes on the wrong one!

Which is which?

have crashed	will understand	invaded
smiled	did not arrive	sing
had promised	buys	had painted
sit	has spotted	
had visited	will drive	

Getting snappy

The photos should be arranged in this order:
Caption A: 1, 2, 3
Caption B: 3, 1, 2
Caption C: 2, 1, 3
Caption D: 2, 3, 1

Pages 80-81

Lost for words

Andrew's desk

He has blown out the candle.
He has broken a glass.
He has eaten an apple.
He has written a letter.
In the afternoon, he blew out the candle.
In the afternoon, he broke a glass.
In the afternoon, he ate an apple.
In the afternoon, he wrote a letter.

Tense trouble

1 They will have to pick up the house before their parents **get back**.
2 Oliver had just finished writing when the examiner **told** them to put down their pens.
3 Lots of people **will visit** the exhibition when it opens next month.
4 I was furious because the train **was** late.
5 She **went** to Hong Kong last year.
6 They **have lived** in New York for two years, and have no plans to move away.

can/may/might

1 I am very glad that Jenny **can** speak French.
2 You **can** spend as much money as you like OR You **may** spend as much money as you like.
3 **Can** I borrow a pencil? OR **May** I borrow a pencil?
4 **May** I phone my parents? OR **Might** I phone my parents?
5 I might go and see a movie this afternoon, if it keeps on raining OR I **may** go and see a film this afternoon, if it keeps on raining.

Pages 82-83

Identity crisis

1 The fridge is full of bacon. (**which I eat everyday**)
2 The ring which he gave me was far too big.
3 The policeman who drove them home was very friendly.
4 My brother is getting married. (**who is a vet**)
5 The boat had been underwater for thirty years. (**which was found by a diver**)

Who or *whom*?

1 The friend with **whom** I went to Egypt has sent me a letter.
2 The people **who** took the other path got there first.
3 Valerie, **who** has just come back from Mexico, speaks fluent Spanish.
4 This is Jo, **whom** I met on the bus OR **who** I met on a bus.

Murder at Snoot Towers

1 which	4 who	7 which
2 who	5 whom	8 whom/that
3 that/which	6 whose	9 that

Hugo Batty murdered Lord Snoot, whom he was blackmailing. Here you can see how he managed to slip unnoticed from the library to the conservatory, by going through the gardens, the nursery and the breakfast room:

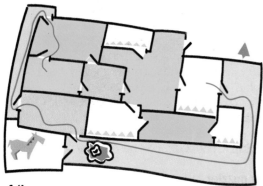

of/'ve

1 "She **must've** decided not to take her car, because I saw it parked in our street this morning."
2 "You really **should've** gone to the party: it was great fun."
3 "We **could've** driven a bit faster, but not much, as the roads are very wet."
4 "If it hadn't been raining, I **would've** come."

Who's who and what's what?

1 The girl **who is swimming** is near the boat.
2 The dog **which is running** has black paws.
3 The ice cream **which the boy is holding** is chocolate and vanilla.
4 The boy **who is running** has red hair.
5 The cow **the policeman is chasing** has black ears.
6 The dog **which is swimming** is near the boat.
7 The baby **the woman is holding** has a pink hat.
8 The man **whom the policeman is chasing** has a red sweater.

Pages 84-85

Comparing climates

1 In August, Weatherchester is **hotter** than Seasonbury.
2 In January, Weatherchester is **colder** than Seasonbury.
3 In March, Seasonbury is **drier** than Weatherchester.
4 In September, Seasonbury is **wetter** than Weatherchester.

Character questionnaire

Jon is more patient than Tessa.
Jon is lazier than Tessa.
Tessa is friendlier than Jon.
Jon is more careful than Tessa.
Tessa is nosier than Jon.
Jon is more selfish than Tessa.

quite/quiet

1 You look **quite** washed out.
2 As Stefan walked **past**, he noticed the man's gun.
3 It is very **quiet** without Diane and Vicky.
4 Veronica was so happy when she **passed** her test.
5 In the **past** week, I have lost two umbrellas.
6 I have always found math **quite** hard.

Moped mania

The Superwhizz is wider than the Pipsqueak.
The Superwhizz is longer than the Pipsqueak.
The Superwhizz is more expensive than the Pipsqueak.
The Superwhizz is faster than the Pipsqueak.
The Superwhizz is heavier than the Pipsqueak.
The Stumbly is wider than the Featherzoom.
The Featherzoom is longer than the Stumbly.
The Featherzoom is more expensive than the Stumbly.
The Featherzoom is faster than the Stumbly.
The Stumbly is heavier than the Featherzoom.
The Thriftyshift is wider than the Pipsqueak.
The Thriftyshift is longer than the Pipsqueak.
The Pipsqueak is more expensive than the Thriftyshift.
The Pipsqueak is faster than the Thriftyshift.
The Pipsqueak is heavier than the Thriftyshift.
The fastest moped Sally can buy is a Pipsqueak.

The Superwhizz is too expensive, and the Featherzoom is too long.

Pages 86-87

in/into

1 He could see a girl diving **into** the pool.
2 Elaine hurried **into** her bedroom.
3 The train had been waiting **in** the tunnel for more than half an hour.
4 We went **into** the garden to look for worms.
5 I lay **in** the bathtub for forty minutes today.

Split conditionals

1. If I had watered the plants, they would not have died.
2. If I water the plants, they will not die.
3. If she pulls my ear, I will bite her.
4. If she pulled my ear, I would have bitten her.
5. If I had run faster, I would have won.
6. If I run faster, I will win.

Dear Maisie

1	will have to	5	were
2	had passed	6	spoke
3	stop	7	will think
4	eat		

A wobbly welcome

Hi folks! Welcome to Costa Boppa! This is the world's most remote island: if you **had come** by boat it would have taken you thirty-nine hours to get here. But it's also the world's most happening hotspot: if you went to the Costa Brava you **would not find** wilder nightlife.

Costa Boppa is simply gorgeous. If you got up at four o'clock, you **would see** some amazing sunrises. If you **want** to explore the island a bit, your Boppa Breaks guide will be happy to arrange a bus tour and cultural extravaganza.

If you come on down to the Boppa Breaks karaoke evening tonight, we **will tell** you more about all the great entertainment lined up for you this week. Well, that's it, folks. If you **have** any questions, just buzz Larry, Carrie or me, Barry, at the Paradise Club.

Pages 88-89

On the record

1. Liz said (that) she had eaten Jo's chocolates the day before yesterday.
2. Bobby asked us what we had done that day.
3. Carol said (that) she was playing squash with her sister that day.
4. Neil asked whether Mandy had borrowed his bike OR Neil asked if Mandy had borrowed his bike.
5. The teacher warned us never to run across the street without looking both ways.

to/too

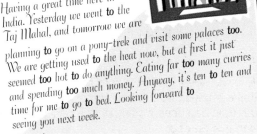

To Ellie,
Having a great time here in India. Yesterday we went **to** the Taj Mahal, and tomorrow we are planning **to** go on a pony-trek and visit some palaces **too**. We are getting used **to** the heat now, but at first it just seemed **too** hot **to** do anything. Eating far **too** many curries and spending **too** much money. Anyway, it's ten **to** ten and time for me **to** go **to** bed. Looking forward **to** seeing you next week.
Much love,
Rob

The Noah C. Parker interview

1. I first decided to be a soap opera star at the age of three.
2. I am working on a new soap opera called Suds and Scandal, all about life at a laundromat.
3. In my spare time I do a lot of yoga and also knit my own sweaters.
4. I am like all celebrities - the life and soul of parties and lots of fun.
5. I have hundreds of friends, but Reginald the rat is great because he never answers back.
6. I hate foreign food and having to shout to make myself understood.
7. One day I will be the most famous person in the world.

Drama in Drabsby

1	had arrived	7	the day before
2	had realized	8	had never left
3	had gone	9	there
4	had never been	10	would have
5	was looking	11	that day
6	had left		

Page 90

The Supertone chair

Ever wanted to look really great?
But not had **any** idea how to lose weight?
Sick of **those** diets and talk of fresh air?
Well, do it at home: buy a Supertone chair!
You don't need to get out **your** jogging suit.
You don't need to eat **any** salads or fruit.
Just sit in your Supertone chair twice a day,
and watch all **those** surplus pounds slip away.
You won't **ever** have looked quite so good, that's for sure.
Nothing **can** work like the Supertone cure.
Enjoy yourself, eat ice cream and cookies.
With the Supertone chair, no one has **any** worries.

Pronoun puzzler

1. Someone has invited **him** and his cousin to go to Japan.
2. You know more about it than **I** do.
3. I hope Gary will dance with **us**.
4. Paula and **I** are going out for lunch.
5. Her brother is almost as tall as **her** (OR **she** - very formal).

A letter home

Dear Ben,
Thanks very much for the comics you sent me: they **were** really funny. My Dad and **I** went ice skating last week, and he kept falling over. I was desperately trying **not to** burst out laughing. My finals start next week, but I'm trying **not to** think about them. Otherwise I don't really have **anything** OR **much** to tell you. Don't forget to send me **those** photos you took when we **were** at the fair last week.
Lots of love,
Lucy

95

This edition was first published in 1997 by Usborne Publishing Ltd, Usborne House, 83-85 Saffron Hill, London, EC1N 8RT, England. www.usborne.com Copyright © 2003, 1997, 1995, 1994. Usborne Publishing Ltd.